REJECTION

A Destiny Stealer

You're SIGNIFICANT, ~~NOT REJECTED~~

TEEN EDITON

by

TIFFANY EALY

ISBN: 979-8-218-95628-8
LCN: 2023912369

Empac Publishing Company

PO Box 1192 Fresno, TX 77545

tiffanyealyspeaks@gmail.com

DEDICATION

Thankful to God THE IAM, Elohim, my wonderful husband, children, in-laws, family, fans, and true friends!

This book is dedicated to my prayer partners who have prayed me through many seasons, and to all those that are suffering some type of rejection, trauma, hurt, pain, and feel unloved, unappreciated, or unworthy. May you all receive the love of God in your heart and come to know his true freedom!

God loves you and says you are Significant & Special!

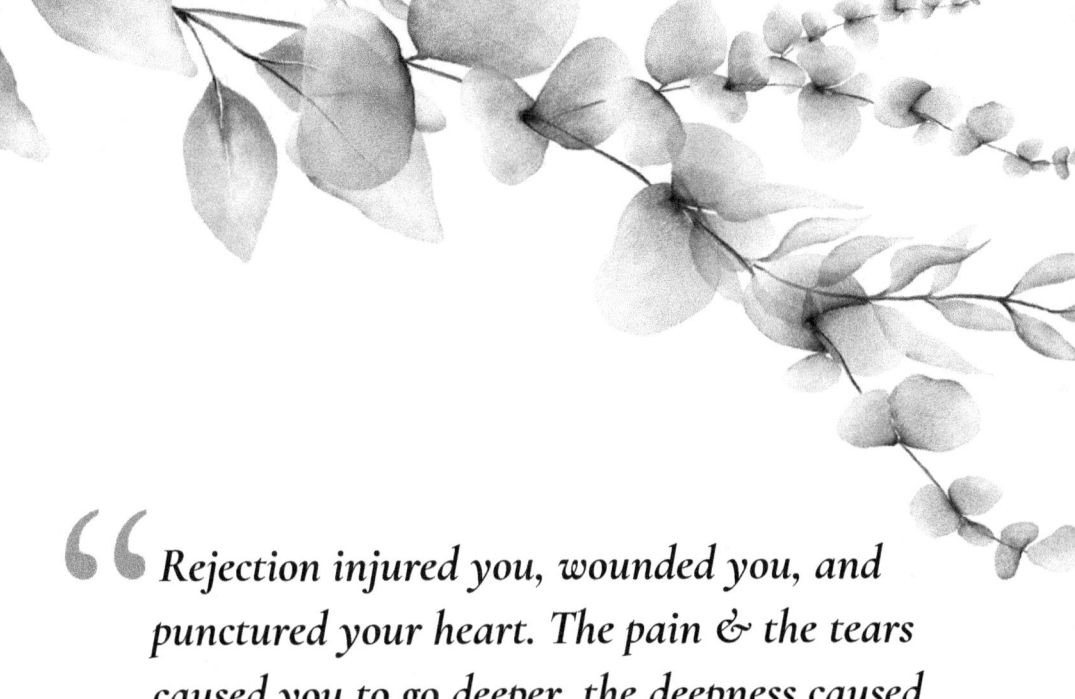

" *Rejection injured you, wounded you, and punctured your heart. The pain & the tears caused you to go deeper, the deepness caused you to know God, Knowing God allowed you to see greatness and know your Power and true Worth!"*

TIFFANY EALY

Table of Contents

Our identity doesn't come from what hurt us nor injured us, but from who created us, loves us and is our true supplier!

TIFFANY EALY

INTRODUCTION

My first book, Jewel Power: Birthing Destiny, is a great awesome written work that speaks about speaking right and discovering purpose and the greatness that God has placed within us. The most important thing about destiny is that before we were formed, God already knew who we would become. He is the creator who made us, equipped us, and placed a great purpose within us. The first thing we must know about ourselves is our position with God. God created each of us as sons and daughters and made us in His own image. He carried all our sins to the cross so that we would have full access to him through His son Jesus. We have full access to the menu; every attribute of heaven is available to us. It is important that we know that when we begin to access purpose, we may have some insecurities and strongholds that have to be healed and made whole. When I started to write my first book, I was on fire and ready to write and be obedient to God. Somewhere along the way, I began to question things, and if I was good enough, and how would others view the book. I began to doubt what God placed within me and also told me to do. I knew what God said was true, but I needed to remove any doubt from my mind and be healed of insecurities. Over the time of seven years, I put the book down and picked it up many times. When I continued to pray, God answered me and said I needed to follow his instructions and get the book out. So, finally, I did and the start of my writing career went forth. This book is about the insecurities, wounds, trauma and

1

strongholds that we carry that attempt to deter our purpose in life. We have to be healed and molded because of many things in life that affect us and attach to our insides that can cause internal damage. Many things may have happened to you in the past, but this is only a part of your story. Your truth is who God says you are and created you to be. You are certainly worthy, special, loved, and significant. You are only fully powerful when you can walk in your truth. The hurt, the pain, and the dirt you went through will be used to deliver someone else. Now, you are ready to be healed from rejection, trauma, and your wounds of the past. Your validation, acceptance, and worth comes from above.

The position that you hold in Christ is exactly who you are meant to be and walk in.

CHAPTER 1
Rejection: A Purpose Stealer

The spirit of rejection is a great enemy that attempts to deter purpose. The spirit of rejection has been around for many before we can remember. Sometimes, rejection attaches to the womb, and our children are born having the spirit of rejection. Think about those in the African American community who were a part of slavery. The ancestors of slavery were called boy, the n-word, beaten and miss-treated, and brain-washed to believe they were beneath other races. The truth is that superiority comes not from race but from our identity as sons and daughters. Our father, the manufacturer, made all of us in His image with different characteristics and talents. The ugliness of rejection can keep individuals from operating in purpose and potential. It can stagnate, cripple and try to shut us down from understanding our truth. Many of us carry rejection within. God states in Isaiah 53:1-5 that Jesus took it to the cross to bring its defeat and demise within our lives. The biggest act of rejection we know is when Jesus Christ was crucified on the cross for our sins. He was rejected, miss-treated, and lied on so that we may have healing and wholeness through him.

Rejection is the opposite of the natural characteristic of being loved, cherished and appreciated for what we do and also who we are. Rejection is a feeling that we are unappreciated, unloved, and undervalued. We are all fearfully and wonderfully made by the creator, and he made us to be loved and in love. Rejection comes certainly to destroy our self-worth, self-esteem, self-image, purpose, and potential. Rejection from others can lead to depression, emotional issues, isolation, fear, intimidation, guilt, and other issues as well.

People who experience rejection normally care about what others say and think about them. Rejected people keep up a shield because they don't feel accepted by others. They sometimes feel like they can never do anything right. Rejected people normally hold feelings within because they don't want to express themselves and be misunderstood. Rejected people can feel entrapped, lonely, and second-guess themselves regularly.

Rejection can come in numerous ways. Oftentimes, it can come from generational curses, parents, friends, family members, teachers, and even self. Once rejection takes root, it allows demonic spirits entry to feed on that person. If not dealt with, rejection will carry forth into your life and it will worsen. The pain can grow and deepen and you don't realize that you are affected. You just feel like this is a part of your life, and it is normal.

Rejection spirits will attach and continue to draw you to more rejection, and it will cause those around you to reject you. You will be rejected by many you know, and also, your job position can be a big place of rejection. The victim will begin to live in expectation that this is who they are, and they will continue to attract the same thing.

When someone gets a physical wound, the wound eventually goes away and you forget it was there. Rejection is that same way, but when it attaches to you, it will grow if not healed. You will rehearse what happened to you and bring more of the same thing to you. Most people respond to what has happened to them in the past. The past has to become a learning tool for us, and we have to move forward. It can't be a place where we allow ourselves to stay. Rejection doesn't allow us to function fully as sons and daughters. It is a constant reminder of how we see ourselves and how we feel others see us. Our society is filled with rejection and trauma that has attached to us.

We really don't even realize that we are dealing with so much because it becomes normal. We learn how to cope and deal with it, but we are not healed. We wear a mask because we are afraid to show up fully because of what others may think about us.

Today, many deal with issues of gender, homosexuality, abandonment and so forth. This is due to some type of rejection issue. The issue may be a generational curse that needs to be broken. God made you exactly perfect, and you were made in his image. He didn't make a mistake with your gender. Jesus chose you to be born on this Earth and chose your Earthly parents. You have a specific identity and fingerprint. It only belongs to you. You should know that your conception was a good thing, and God wanted you to be here. You are here on purpose and for a purpose. God knows your name and your identity. You are a blessing and not a mistake.

Prayer

God, You created every part of us. You placed us together in the womb. You wrote our destiny in the books of heaven. You knew us by name and every attribute of our being. Lord shape our thoughts to coincide with Your thoughts of us. Let us delight in our being. Lord may Your precious thoughts fill us with delight and happiness of our being.

I can remember others describing their childhood and events that occurred. I realized that some of the memories of my childhood I probably suppressed. I had forgotten so many memories along the way. God would allow me to remember certain things I had not thought about in years. This is what sometimes happens when Trauma hits. We begin to hide behind the hurt and pain and suppress things. Especially when we have some things in our childhood that may be sad. Overall, I am thankful that I had a great childhood and wonderful friends. Rejection is an evil spirit and it is not of God. It is not an emotion, but it lives within us if we allow it to enter. Today, I speak to any broken part of your life that felt any rejection. You are loved, wanted, and appreciated by God. Know that God wants you to choose him and not the spirit of rejection. His spirit revives, heals, sets free, and delivers. Everything you need can be found in Jesus Christ. He doesn't want you to carry any hurt or pain with you.

Your Truth

" *You are wonderfully made by the manufacturer.*

PSALMS 139:4

" *God created each of us for a purpose; We are special, unique, and significant.*

JEREMIAH 29:11

CHAPTER 2
Your True Source

God is our true source, and our identity comes from God. God loves us and knows everything about us, from beginning to end. God doesn't make any mistakes. He created some male and some female, so that reproduction can take place and we multiply the Earth. God makes no mistakes, so don't question His creation. He made you perfect. The world's ways will have you question your identity, but if you know the Father, you will know who you are. The world suffers from homosexuality and gender issues. This is rejection. Our identity is not a mistake; it is perfect. We will have disappointments in life, especially if we place our trust in man. Man is unable to see the heart and know everything about God's creation. The creator that created us as sons and daughters knows everything about us.

We must seek the will and the ways of the Father, so we can walk in trueness. Man will fail, we will fail, but God will never fail us or fail. He is infallible and His ways are perfect and just.

When we are children, we are born into this world to our parents chosen by God to cover us. The thing is, sometimes, our parents have been mishandled and mistreated and carry rejection as well. This allows us to become lost and filled with many questions. The answer will always be Jesus Christ. Our true identity comes from above. Our identity is influenced oftentimes by school, jobs, family members, traditions, church, etc. The influence sometimes may be good, but it can also be harmful as well. When we are young, we think about making good grades, playing, eating, and our friends. We develop a personality based on the things around us. This is why it is so important for us to encourage our children, speak the right words, and believe in the source. Our source has to be Jesus Christ because if we hold the world as the source, we will fail. The things of the world have us to think that many wrong things are actually right because it is in our face and seems that way. We must always know that the true source never changes; only technology and the way we receive the information. Jesus is still the I AM, The all-powerful, all-knowing and the only answer.

We are not capable of walking in true identity without knowing our true worth that comes from above. It is essential to know our Father and to consult Him for our purpose. The more we connect with the Father the more He will communicate with us regarding our life and purpose. He will speak to us and also speak life over us, and He constantly interceded for us in heaven. Our prayers are heard, and we must speak life and activate heaven for our purpose. Our purpose is already written, but we must move forward and activate it with our words.

We were made to be divinely connected to the source. We should activate heaven and communicate with the source daily and regularly. If we can make time for other things, we should be able to make time for the source where all things come from, including us. Our Father wants us to live rejection-free, and in wholeness and freedom. He wants us to know that through our covenant, rights, healing and wholeness are available. What the enemy may have meant for our downfall, God wants to turn it around for our good. According to Romans 8:28 NLT, and we know that God causes everything to work together for the good of those who love God." This is our proof, whatever pain, dirt and harm we go through, God will use it for our testimony and for his glory. Our pain is necessary and it will help those assigned to us. When we are wounded, we operate in a place of stagnation and we feel stuck. This holds us down and makes us feel like we can't move forward. For this reason, we must access our source so we can experience healing and wholeness. It is certainly true that people will hurt us and reject us. If we know who we are, we do not have to accept it is truth. We can rebuke those offenses and not allow them to attach to us. The thing is hurt; people will continue to hurt others. Many people are hurt and damaged and don't even know they are.

Your Truth

God doesn't show favoritism. He loves all His children and thinks we are special!

Man can fail us but, God never fails us. God wants the best for His children, and He wants us to know our Purpose and walk it in boldly.

ROMANS 2:11

Reject thoughts and words contrary to God's word!

PSALMS 139:4 , 1 PETER 2:4

CHAPTER 3

Rejection From Trauma

Trauma happens when something out of the ordinary and horrific disturbs your life. One of the most traumatic events I went through was losing my father as a child. I can remember, I was only eight years old; my father was battling diabetes and in coma for weeks. We went to church daily, we prayed and it seemed like nothing was happening. I knew that this time he was not going to come through this coma. Our time with him on Earth was near. This was real; I was about to lose my earthly father. As a child, this is devastating. I always cared about my grades, but during this time, I didn't want to study. After the first year, I began to feel better and stronger each day.

I never lost hope in God, but I questioned so many things. This was certainly an experience that you would not wish on anyone. I thought about the many things that my father would miss in my life. I also thought about the memories and the time God had given him to us. This was the first trauma that I had gone through, and I didn't know how to heal from it.

After many years, I remember my mom finally decided she would begin to date. She had assured us that she didn't want to get married again. I wanted her to be happy again and fulfilled, and I knew she had gone through so much pain. What I didn't anticipate is how her dating would affect our lives. I did not anticipate how we would feel and if we would like him. Would we be like a blended family? Then, after she started dating, I realized that her time was spent dating and pleasing another man that wasn't my father. I didn't anticipate that her time would be spent with him a lot. I remember one of her relationships, and his wife had actually died. In this relationship, my mom was now a step-mom. She would now be a mother figure to his son. She would attend his games and be present as much as possible. At this point, I didn't realize how important it was for her to be present at our events. I realized that this is the first time I felt some type of way. I didn't know what the feelings were called and what I was experiencing. I just felt that something didn't seem right about this. As time went on, I was growing older and my friends and school-work filled my time more and more. I stayed busy with Piano, Band and many other things. It wasn't until my adult life that God brought back to my attention. This is where parts of my rejection started. Like so many others, I had carried pain from losing my father and rejection into my adult life. This is why I had felt rejected in many other occurrences in my life.

Death and violence are two things that can cause trauma. Of course, other things like rape, abuse, police brutality, racism can also cause trauma. These are the type of things that we must be healed from. We must know who we are and know God so that we can be whole. A life without knowing father, we will live beneath his standards for our life. God doesn't want us to live from a place of trauma and pain but from a place of purpose and wholeness.

I remember, after college, I was working a second job at a nightclub. I received a call, and I just was in utter shock. I received a phone call that my brother, nephew, that his wife had shot them and herself. I didn't know a status, but I knew I had to drive quickly to the hospital. I got to the hospital emergency room, and I found out my nephew had passed away and didn't make it. This was like something in the movies that you never think would happen to your family. I could not believe what I had just heard. I couldn't imagine what my brother was going through. She wanted to kill the whole family. God had different plans, and she and my brother lived. She was pregnant with another son at the time. The baby was fine, but of course, the baby would experience things in the womb from all the distress. This was devastating to the core. You wonder why this occurred, and you don't know what others carry within. This was certainly not an act of God, and a stronghold needed to be broken.

I could not understand or judge her, but I just prayed that she would come to know Christ fully and receive healing and salvation. The strongholds we carry, rejection and wounds, can be dangerous if not dealt with. The only antidote is to keep moving forward and know that God still has a purpose in the destruction.

These two traumatic times certainly hurt to the core. I would not wish any of this on anyone. One thing I do know is that God is still who He says He is. As I wrote my first book, God revealed to me times where I experienced rejection. This was when I realized that I held rejection within. He began to heal my wounds and heart and make me whole. As I was healing, I realized that my stagnant times is when the rejection caused havoc and attempted to keep me down. The pains of rejection are often carried by many, but we don't diagnose it or know it is there. We just know how we feel but don't acknowledge the act of rejection. We can't fully be healed until we acknowledge and know the root of our pain and feelings. God is able to heal every insecurity, pain, hurt and wound within if you seek Him and allow Him. He wants each of us to walk in the fullness of freedom and wholeness. Our full purpose and potential can't go forth without dealing with our feelings and insecurities.

Pathways Rejection Enters

- Rejection can enter by an unwanted pregnancy
- Rejection can enter by a child out of wedlock
- Thoughts of Abortion
- Accidents, Trauma
- Alcohol dependency
- Divorce
- Drugs
- Financial Hardships
- Mistaken Pregnancy
- Abandoned Father or Mother
- Long Labor
- Medicines that cause depression
- Wanted different gender
- Prolonging Naming the Child
- Words of Offense Spoken, Negative Words
- Bullying

Your Truth

" *God will use the pain and the dirt that tried to deter you for His glory and your testimony!*

" *God can heal every insecurity, pain and hurt!*

PSALMS 147:3

CHAPTER 4
Tradition & Rejection

There are many church homes in our communities and we can see them as we drive just in our area. There are many denominations, rules, and regulations that the church teaches us. Traditions and rules and beliefs can be a hindrance to our walk. I say this because we are led to Christ normally by our parents and we attend church with them. We begin to develop our understanding of God by what we are taught from our church foundation. Jesus Christ was rejected by many, lied on, and bruised for our sins. He knew truth and taught truth, but many were led by rules, opinions and interpretations of what they thought was true. They didn't realize they had truth walking right before them. This is why we must seek to understand and know Christ for ourselves. As I grew older, I always believed but knew there was more. I decided to pursue a true relationship with the father. I can recall sitting in church with my mother at a Catholic service. The priest didn't speak English well and I could not understand anything. My mother fell asleep in service; I believe she was snoring. This was when I knew I needed to know God for myself. This was when I made the decision to step out and seek God and his fullness.

I needed more, and this was not working for me. Furthermore, we had been divided in our walk as children because my father had switched to Baptist. We went to church with my father on holidays and special occasions as a family. We had become separated in hearing God's word as a family. My father was getting fed one place, and we were in another denomination. We serve one God, but each denominations views were different and the rules were different. After reading my Bible more and seeing the miracles of God, I realized that none of those miracles were going on near me. I wanted to see God's Spirit and hand move. I realized that every church didn't hold the spirit or believe in prophecy or miracles. I needed to experience more, and I was ready to pursue just that.

I remember a God moment when I first met Apostle Martin in the beauty shop. She was ministering in the beauty shop and was so pleasant. She introduced herself and told me about her groundbreaking for her new church. She saw that I was pregnant, and she prayed over my belly for my unborn son. I saw the God within her. At the time, we lived in Texas. We went to church, but I had not found the right church home. About a year later, we moved to Louisiana and attended Divine Grace Temple. This church was exactly what I had been wanting to experience. It was radical and led by the spirit of God. Apostle Martin spoke life and prophetically and believed in miracles.

One of the greatest things, she was a giver and sower. She opened our understanding that God's giving occurs through us. We had been givers of the past, but she brought out more in us and spoke into our lives. Many of the miracles that God wants to perform, He wants to do through us. This is where our new journey began. She told us so many stories of starting a ministry with her husband and how much my husband and I reminded her of them. These memories are priceless to us. I now understood that God was doing something great within our lives. God had brought us to a church home that we felt comfortable and also where we could grow. Then, it was evident that I was changing and my belief system was coming into truth. The more I studied and sought God, the more I grew. Some of my family thought that I had joined a cult because I had left the Catholic faith. I should not have to defend the God I serve because we both serve God. We should be able to recognize God in others if we know God. The denomination is not what matters, but what truly matters is knowing the presence of God. We should know the attributes of God and who God is. Only then can we recognize that we are made in His image and there is only one true God. God is a God of love and goodness. God is not concerned with our denomination but our heart and obedience to Him. I was growing in my faith, but my faith was also being tested and I experienced rejection once again. Then, it was like Apostle Martin knew what was going on. I went to Bible Study and she called me up for prayer. She hugged me tight and said, :you need a Mother's Hug and I want to pray for you.: Yes, God knew exactly what I needed. She said, what you are going through; God will use for His glory. Stay strong. God always knows what we need and is there when we need Him.

I recall a time when one of my friends was going through a rough patch. God revealed that I needed to pray with her daily and go on a fast with her. I knew that this fast is what she needed to get through, and I was obedient to the fast. Little did I know, God was doing something in me while He was healing her. He allowed me to learn how others reject us because they have been rejected. He allowed me to understand that the root of rejection came from deeper in the family line. This was an eye-opener to me that allowed me to look at things very differently. Of course, it helped her to get through her rough time and trust God at His word. One thing, we knew that God was working on both of us. He certainly loves his children, and he will provide exactly what you need. (Intentional God) God cares about everything that happens to us.

Tradition can be harmful if we continue to make decisions on tradition and not obedience. If we are obedient to God, we break cycles and strongholds. This, of course, is not easy to do because with obedience, there is resistance and opposition. The great thing is that with obedience comes healing, blessing, and open doors for generational blessings to flow. We can't follow tradition if it deters and hinders our truth and purpose. We are truly called by God to be Earth Shakers and Curse Breakers. We have to place a halt to what is trying to control our lives, especially when it alters our identity. Our identity is meant to allow us to walk in power and greatness, not stagnation and limitations. We have to choose obedience and sacrifice because it is our truth and our identity relies on it.

I can remember when my family first saw me coming to know Christ in a greater capacity. I was accused of being a part of a cult. I was also asked if I only wore dresses. Now mind you, it was full swing summer and I had a pair of shorts on and a t-shirt. I just laughed it off and rebuked the comment that was mentioned. Of course, I am sure there was much more said, but others don't fully understand your path with God. This is a major way in which traditions and denominations can harm your perception of Christ. This is why it is so vital to know Christ for yourself. We must know our position in Christ and also have a relationship with Christ. The more we seek Christ, and He works through us and in us, we find out more about our father. We come to know how good He is and how much He cares about His children. We come to trust in Christ and not man.

Your Truth

" *You are accepted and endorsed by God!*

EPHESIANS 3:19

" *God wants to set us free from bondage, soul-ties and harm!*

LUKE 4:18

CHAPTER 5
Words Are Our Sword

Words are so important, they can speak life and they can also speak death. They can uplift or deter. Many of us don't think about our words carefully before we speak. This occurs to us even more when we are upset or angry and we speak out quickly from emotions. Words of offense can be spoken by many people in our lives that are attached to us. When words of offense take root, they can cause pain, stagnation, and cause us to question ourselves. For instance, I have heard many people say I was always getting into things, and a family said I would never be anything. We have to watch our words and pray that our loved ones become who God called them to be. We have to watch our words because they can attach to that person, ourselves and our children. We were never thought that we truly need to watch our words. Words attach to us, especially when we are dealing with rejection. Our identity is altered and we are getting our worth from others and not God. This is why we must know who we are in Christ so that we can combat the offense with the word. If we are not careful, we will allow what others speak to be truth in our life. God only intends for us to accept His truth, and not what others think as truth.

Words can hurt, and actions can hurt that are done to us and cause us to rehearse over and over in our mind. This is what causes us to hold unforgiveness and resentment within. We feel rejected and have allowed the offense to take hold within our lives. We don't realize how we can stagnate purpose in others by the words we say and our actions. The enemy will use many close to us to bring rejection and offense that cause us to feel stuck and stagnated. This is why we truly have to have a relationship with the father. When rejection goes unhealed, it will enter into our friendships, relationships, marriage, workplace, and our everyday lives. When someone offends us and we hold unforgiveness. We have to truly seek the father to forgive ourselves and others. When we hold onto unforgiveness, it opens doors for sickness, stagnation and continues to hinder our purpose. We have to let God be the judge and let go. Forgiveness doesn't mean we have to rekindle the friendship or relationship, but it does mean we need to love and pray for them. We have to forgive so we are set free, and God can continue to move in our lives. God doesn't want anything to stagnate us and take our focus off of him. Holding resentment, rejection and other offenses take our focus off of God and His attributes. When we truly know our identity, we can combat offense and rejection with the word of God. We have to walk in truth, and not accept the lies and plot of the enemy to prevail.

Vows can be strongholds to us because we spoke something with our mouths. Remember, your mouth allows heaven to answer. This is why our parents would say don't swear about anything. Sometimes we open our mouths to try and protect ourselves from offense. For example, someone that has been injured by a relationship. They speak I will never love again, and get married. Later on, of course, they forget they ever spoke this. Then, when they are ready to love again, they wonder;

"why am I not finding the right mate." Now, this horrific vow they have spoken is to be undone. Vows and our words can keep us from our future and moving ahead. This is why we must be aware of our words because they can hinder ourselves and others. Think about it, would you want to speak anything that harms someone from moving forward. I hope your answer was no. We should not want to hinder or deter purpose in ourselves or others. We make vows to suppress our emotions and hurt. We must be aware of our words because they shape us, mold us, and create in our lives. Our only mechanism to combat hurt is to be truly healed from the pain, speak God's word and know our true worth.

I remember going through a rough time, and I had felt some type of way because of offensive words. I remember God revealing to me that every time I went over the water, he was releasing pain and wounds. This was profound to me; I now imagine that the blood and the water are always cleansing me from hurt. You will go through things; you do things where people say things or do something that offends us. It is life. We must always remember that our father is with us, and we are who God says. Secondly, he has given us his word as a weapon. The Holy Spirit is our guide and is always there to guide us in times of trouble. God has established a new covenant with His children and all old things are gone, and he wants us to walk in our truth. Your new identity lies in Christ, your greatest asset and relationship. You are who God says you are, and He is the healer and supplier of every need.

Your Truth

" Words hurt if we take offense and allow them in, we must combat the offense and use His word as our weapon!

" Reject every thought that is contrary to what God's word says!

CHAPTER 6
Rejection in Relationships

When we experience rejection, we carry rejection within and our relationships are affected. We carry rejection in our workplace, marriage, relationships and friendships and family life. Sometimes, we become offended easily because we already have the wounds within. We cry easily because we are already broken and trying to figure out why others perceive us and reject us. We wonder why we attach to relationships that are broken because we carry rejection. We become easily offended because we allow offense to seep in easily and attach to us. Many times people that feel rejection feel they are not good enough or worthy. They feel like they easily make mistakes. The perception of these thoughts they have causes them to receive more feelings of not good enough and failure. When we are not healed within, we receive more of the same. The rejection grows until we seek healing and help from God.

In the workplace, sometimes we are rejected by others and our bosses. Can you think of a time where you were passed over for a position? You know you were qualified and had the education, but someone else received the promotion. This is a feeling of rejection that can harm us from moving forward. In the workplace, we have to understand that our job is to be done unto God. God is the supplier of our job and all our needs. Yes, we may have been mistreated and mishandled, but God will open doors for us and provide justice. We must know that if we continue to do our job unto God, the right doors and the right opportunities will open up. If God says yes, then no one can change the decision. This is why it is important for us to decree things and speak forth our destiny. We must continue to speak the word of God and not allow the issues of this world to become bigger than the God we serve. What happens to us does not have to make us bitter, but it should make us better. We have to continue to stay rooted and grounded in his word because rejection happens in life. It is not always easy, but our focus has to be on God and not man. How we handle the rejection is key to us receiving what God has for us. Look at it this way, God has a greater door for you to walk through, and he may have closed the door to the promotion.

The enemy will try to attack you through rejection when a storm has come into your life. You are down and out and trying to figure things out. This is a time when you need those close to you to provide love and nurturing. This is a time when you even want your spouse to understand what you are going through. God didn't make us to feel validated by others, but he wants us to seek His love and His will. This is the time when even our spouse can't give us what we need. God wants us to seek Him as our father and know that he is the healer and provider of every need. Rejection can cloud your judgment and cause you to second-guess things. I can remember a time when I wanted to go back to work. It seemed like that door would not open up. I knew I had a lot of education and interviewed well. I was trying to stay focused and motivated. It wasn't until I surrendered to God and changed my prayer that I felt freedom. I realized that God wanted me to release my first book, and I hadn't done it. I was sitting on my purpose because of fear. I had to repent, and I began to be truly healed of my insecurities. God sent answers and began to download to me once again. It is hard to hear from God when you feel rejected and stagnant. I went on a fast, and I began to speak life over myself and my books. Yes, I said books; I knew there were many more books in me than the first one. Why, because God had said it. This is why it is so important to stay rooted and grounded in His word.

God is the source of our identity. When we look for validation and acceptance from others, we will feel rejected and lost. We will not always get the acceptance we need nor the validity. We sometimes take on a false identity because of relationships with our parents, friends, and others we are connected to. Not even our labels or job position define us. We can lose a position or a label. We must solve the identity crisis. The crisis within ourselves that plague many because we look to music, the world and others to validate us. Our true validation can only come from the manufacturer. He made us with original parts, and no one has our fingerprint. What happens to us is often not our fault; how we handle it is what matters. Our identity is at stake, and our truth. We are made to be wealthy, powerful, and strong, but we can't allow mammon to cloud our minds as to who our supplier is. Everything we have belongs to God, and our identity comes from God. God is the one that gives us the ability to obtain wisdom, our anointing and riches. This is something we must always remember. We must never compromise who we are for money because our true source is our supplier. The only validation we need comes from above, and we must seek His will.

Bullying is something that has become more common now than ever. I remember back in the day; the bully wanted your lunch or money for lunch because they were hungry. Now, the bully attacks the way you look, dress, act, and how you perceive yourself. I often wonder, if the bully could see the future person, would they attack that person's character. Rejection from bullying can be fatal to young children. It can devalue them and diminish their self-worth. The person being bullied often feels they have to people-please. They don't feel like they can stand up for themselves. They lose security early in who they are. It is so important that we speak to our children about speaking right and taking up for others. The words that they speak and the actions they make can change someone's life or save a life. Bullying is certainly not cool and not of God.

Oftentimes when people go through rejection and pain in relationships, they turn to something else. This may be drinking, drugs, video games, music, fornication and other ways we find to cope. They are looking for love in relationships and idols that are never going to heal the pain. The problem is you have to keep finding solutions because the pain will not go away. The only answer is the Exodus. Jesus Christ is our way and our truth. What we repeat and continue to put a band-aid on doesn't get healed. Only the word, the blood and the father can heal the wounds of rejection and trauma. Until we seek the Father and His mighty hand of healing, we will seek more of the same validation from idols and man. Our relationships will hurt and never seem to provide what we need in our life. We will continue to bleed out, cry out until we seek the healer. Our relationships and experiences are affected by our thoughts and thought patterns. When we develop wrong thoughts about ourselves and seek validation in man. We will always feel like we are miss-treated and miss-handled. The thing is,

God wants to mold and mend every broken area and set us agree. He is the healer and wants to pour over His power into us.

One of my favorite Psalms 23:3, : He restoreth my soul, and guides me into paths of righteousness for His name's sake. He refreshes and restores my soul (life) and leads me in the right paths. (guidance) The true relationship we need in our lives starts with the father. When we understand who He is, then we can establish strong, healthy relationships with others. Why, because then we have an understanding of our position, identity, and our worth. Only when we know our worth will we value ourselves and not abuse our identity.

Prior to writing this book, God began to place the burden on my heart deeply and began to show me so many people that had been mishandled and rejected. He began to send people to me that had experienced rejection in many areas of their life. It was like I could actually feel their pain and hurt. God used me on many occasions to pray for others experiencing rejection and to speak life into them. It was then that I began to understand that this book was very important and that lives needed to be changed. I began to understand the importance of writing this book and helping others to heal and be set free. Each of us has an assignment from God and many are waiting on our purpose to help them walk in their purpose.

CHAPTER 7
Rejection Injects Fear

Rejection alters your identity where you view yourself in a manner that is beneath how God created you to operate. It violates the heart and character of a person. The person views themselves as inadequate, underappreciated, undervalued, and fearful at times. It causes a bruise on the person's heart. Rejection makes a person view themselves and see themselves based on appreciation and validation. This is why many begin to fear how others think of them and accept them. While some may rebel and act out in opposition, aggressive behavior and defiance.

Some may self-reject themselves because they feel insecure, intimidated and inadequate. Still, others may self-protect themselves by building walls and isolate themselves in fear. All these things can keep us from walking in our identity. It can hold us back from our truth. The fear of not being accepted or perceived and accepted can also hold us back. The truth is that the enemy wants to control our creativity and our purpose, so we do not achieve full potential.

The enemy wants to shut our mouths and shut down our worth. This is why we have to think about the promise and stay grounded in God.

God's plan is so important and vital to us becoming powerful and everything we need to be in life for ourselves and to help others. I don't know about you, but I owe it to myself to see purpose live out and come forth in my life. I need all of God's goodness, and I want to see others free and walking in truth as well. I want to live full and see heaven activated on Earth before I leave this world. If we all allow fear to stifle us and lock up our dreams, what God has for us will die. God gives us a choice to live in his truth or choose our own path. You are fully equipped right now to walk in your purpose. God gives us a spirit of boldness and confidence that we may do so. The greatness within you will be unlocked as you take a step forward in faith. Seek God's fullness and deliverance today. He is the healing elixir that will heal every wall and dark spot. Sickness, pain, and hurt can't live where God dwells. Fear and worry can also bring forth sickness in your body. The mind, body, and spirit are connected. With rejection, we can experience fear, bitterness, angriness, anxiety, and other feelings that lead to sickness. Strokes, heart attacks, diabetes, arthritis, skin disorders, mental health, ulcers, and many other sicknesses can all be caused by rejection issues. Rejection can cause heavy stress in your life that may cause panic attacks. The inner conflict in your life causes a reaction and it comes forth in a panic attacks.

I remember reading that someone wrote, if you sick, ask who is wrong with them? It is not what is wrong, but who did you wrong that matters. We must be careful to go to God instantly and speak his word over our lives to combat the offense and wrong feelings. It is said by doctors that injury from trauma and rejection is not much different from physical injury. It can actually be worse if you rehearse the pain and it continues to grow. We have to deal with identity issues. Those issues can take root mostly on the inside, but they can also show up in our outer appearance. We must access the Father and the healer so we can heal inside until it shows up on the outside.

Once God heals you, you can begin to smile again, shine again, and live freely again. Fear is not a characteristic of God. We must truly trust our father that he is well capable of removing our fear and doubts. Doubts come forth because of the way we perceive ourselves. We must think highly of ourselves and know that God is our biggest cheerleader that wants us to succeed. The God we serve will uphold us in his hands, so we won't miss a beat. We have to stay rooted and grounded in the promises and the word of God. If God said it, we can be rest assured that it will come forth. His track record is perfect and without flaws. We don't have to worry about the how, when, or if. God will make sure your promises prevail. We have to turn in every situation to God, knowing that He is bigger than any storm, situation, or event. God can't fail, and if we fall. God will catch us and open a new door. Our faith has to grow beyond our fear. Our belief in God's abilities has to be superior to that of man. Have the God-confidence today that you will not fear anymore. You are able to shine forth and move higher in the greatness God has for you. Let the fear of rejection die within because God is not a God of fear. God says you are worthy, significant, special, gifted, smart, chose and certainly more than enough.

Your Truth

" Your faith is your evidence of God's word, that once you move forward, manifestation shall come forth!

" God has redeemed you, I have called you by name; You are mine!

ISAIAH 43:1

" God provides and equips us with confidence and boldness that delivers us from our fears. You are ready for battle and for greatness!

PSALMS 34:4-5

CHAPTER 8
Over-Comer

Many of us are familiar with the story of Joseph in the Bible. He was one of Jacob's twelve sons. His father loved him more than any of the others and gave him a colored cloak. Of course, his brothers were jealous of him and hated their brother. Additionally, Joseph had many dreams from God that fore-shadowed what was going to come forth. I am sure his brothers did not understand the dreams, but they knew that Joseph carried favor and was unique. Next, the brothers plotted against Joseph and had him sold into slavery. He was taken to Egypt and eventually became a steward to Potiphar and one of Pharaoh's officials. Now Joseph had to feel some type of way about being sold and rejected by his brothers. Joseph was away from all his family and had no family with him. This had to be very hard and hurtful. I am sure Joseph had some sessions where he cried and questioned God. The thing that is so awesome is that Joseph went through some tests and trials but stayed grounded and rooted in the promises. Joseph was very focused and did not want to diminish his name nor position. In the end, thankfully, Joseph forgave to his family for what they had done. He did not keep any bitterness that would alter his promise. Joseph was able to walk in the promise, and even his family that disowned him was able to reap the benefits of his faithfulness. This is a great example of God's goodness and faithfulness.

When God gives us a promise, He will reveal to us pieces of the promise. It is important that when storms come to oppose the promise, we stand on God's word. I can remember having a dream where I was flying high and so fast that I had no control. Every time I wanted to throw in the towel and stop writing, God will bring back this dream to me. Another dream I had, I was going up a spiral staircase and it is was moving upward. I got to the middle and a floor, and I could hear a voice say, "you are going all the way to the top floor." When God has an assignment for you, He will remind you of the promise. We have to make the promise and helping others greater than our fear. God has made us to be powerful overcomers and receivers of his goodness. We have a covenant right to his goodness that is binding. In times where we feel pain, broken, let down, and trauma comes we have to know that God wants us to be healed and free. We have to call on the name of Jesus because it is the name above all names that will give us breakthrough and freedom.

Now, the greatest story of betrayal was when Judas Iscariot, one of the twelve apostles betrayed his master. The act of the crucifixion and death of Jesus Christ. Judas actually kissed Jesus to identify him. This story is known as one of the biggest stories of disloyalty. During the crucifixion, Jesus was beaten, ridiculed, spit-on, and treated harshly. This powerful story of betrayal was a necessary part of Jesus Christ becoming our eternal high priest and intercessor in heaven. Little did Judas know, God's plan was going forth and Jesus would be resurrected on the third day. Due to this betrayal, we now have a binding covenant and inheritance in heaven. We are now under the new covenant where we share so many rights. Here are just a few to name. We have full access to the menu of heaven. It is our birthright and can't be taken away.

- Salvation
- Healing
- Prosperity
- Deliverance
- Freedom
- Joy
- Strength
- Peace
- Righteousness
- Protection
- Holy Spirit

Now you know that you serve a powerful God, and if He is able to heal me and others, He will do it for you too. First, you have to acknowledge your feelings to God and seek His help. Secondly, know who you are in Christ and the attributes of heaven. Thirdly, Pray, Fast, and speak and decree life over yourself daily. Speak the truth and what God's word says about you. His spoken word is a great weapon that we have if we use it. The word creates and it is also a way to be set free. Now, offense and rejection may still try and come to hinder your walk. You must continue to combat it with the word of God. Who God has set free is free indeed, we must rebuke the enemy and the enemy will flee. Deny rejection the opportunity to have authority in your life anymore. Make God ruler and also remember you are an overcomer through the blood.

Today, it is time to divorce rejection and tell it to go. Let rejection know you are finished and will not accept it to dwell any longer. Tell it goodbye and shut the door now. Your ruler is Jesus Christ and you are free. Come out of any agreement with the enemy of trauma and rejection. Your promise is too big to allow rejection or trauma to dwell within. As you break rejection off of you, it shall also be broken off your offspring. You have to exercise your God-given authority. God gave us authority to use and not abuse. Now, God may begin to download times where you felt rejected. Give all the hurt and pain to God. Let Him heal every broken area.

Today, I believe that you are getting set free. You have taken the first step and believe that God will move on your behalf. The pain of rejection, trauma and other strongholds that you went through was necessary. God will use your pain for His glory and to help others. There are some assigned to you that you need to help heal. Remember who you are in Christ and know you are an OVERCOMER through Christ, The Elohim, The healer, The Great I AM loves you and will never leave you! Move your feet and push ahead towards the promise. Align your mind with God's word. You have to fully change your mind to leave the past behind and place now and future as your mission. You have permission from God to move ahead and prepare for greater. Operate from a position of now and moving forward. God will show himself mightily in your life. He is all you need!

CHAPTER 9
Dream/ Final Words

As I was writing this book, I was awakened to a vivid dream. I was not sure about what the dream meant until I began to seek the Holy Spirit's guidance. In the dream, there was a line of people that seemed to never stop. The line was ongoing to where you would have to be patient in line to get to the front of the line. Every person that entered the line had a security mechanism on the items they purchased. This was when God showed me our destiny is secure in Him, and it is locked until we begin to pursue it and unlock what is within us. However, there are deterrents like rejection, trauma, pain, opposition, and fear that will come and try to block your true destiny. In the dream, every person that arrived at the counter was unlocked to be free to walk in destiny. Today, seek the father and leave everything behind. Tell every purpose blocker that is hindering you it is time to go. (BYE) It is now time to be unlocked and walk in the fullness of potential and power. Make it a priority to seek the Father, so your validation comes from Him and not man. From this day, your identity shall be rooted in the father and no one else. You are made to be fully aware and powerful of who you are!

As I wrote my first book, I was on fire for God. I was excited but also fearful still. I wondered if it would be accepted. That woman that began that book is not who I am now. I was a lover of Christ but still not fully aware of my truth. Now, I release to you that if God healed me, He can do it for you. I know that I am good enough, worthy and that there are some that need to read this book. I know that my voice needs to be heard. I am now proud to be called a child of Christ and proud of who He called me to be. I have a purpose that is great, powerful and I also want others to walk in their true worth and power. I no longer care who talks about me, or what they think. I know what my father thinks and says about me. I am chosen, significant, and special to my Father. I know that I carry an anointing that needs to be shared with others. I now can hold my head high and smile with joy, and I know I am exactly who I was called to be. I have the love of God within me. This woman has been made whole and no longer apologizes for being who she is. I am unapologetically me.

I have discovered the me factor. I chase purpose and live with a purpose. I encourage you to find peace within that only comes from God alone. Ask the father who you are in him? He certainly will reveal who He made you to be. There is only one person that knows the answer, the manufacturer, THE ELOHIM. He is the creator of you and all that is. There are no words to describe when you have peace and can walk in your true destiny. The gifts and promises of God can't be brought. They are inherited. The greatest inheritance you can have. Don't waiver, don't lose your smile. Remember, God made only one you, and He made you to be powerful and whole. You have enough faith; just remember to believe like Crazy that your Father is who He says and will do what he says. Block out the doubts, and leave the naysayers behind. Your promise is great and it is already prepared and waiting. Don't get upset; your Judas is necessary in order for you to grow and thrust forward. When you see Judas, remember the blessing is coming forth.

You will be able to thank your opposition later. The opposition brings forth true strength and fortitude. God will truly show you how strong and powerful you are. What was meant for your demise shall be turned around for Him glory. You are truly made by Elohim to win, prosper and be great! Be free, Go forth and possess your promise!

CHAPTER 10
Signs, Decrees, Prayers

Signs of Rejection

- Being Avoided
- Overlooked
- Neglected
- Cold Shoulder
- Shunned by Friends
- Denial
- Ignored

Curses of Rejection

- Failed Relationships
- Divorce
- Loss of Jobs
- Health Issues
- Teen Pregnancy
- Abuse
- Control

Inner Feelings

- Anxiety
- Worry
- Panic Attacks
- Guilt
- Depression
- Disappointment
- Un-fulfillment
- Despair
- Fear
- Loss
- Inadequate
- Un-happy
- Sadness
- Lonely
- Negativity
- Low Self-Esteem
- Worthless Feeling
- Fear of Other's Opinion
- Un-appreciated
- Perfection
- Shame
- Condemnation of Self

Outward Signs

- Anger
- Rebellion
- Aggressive Attitudes
- Anger
- Argumentative
- Arrogance
- Fighting
- Pride
- Refuse affection
- Un-belief
- Vengeful
- Bitter
- Un-forgiveness
- Control
- Foul Language
- Hardness
- Stubborn
- Want to Prove Self
- Reject others

Mirror Exercise

Now pray and ask God, at what point in your life did you experience rejection? If it was as a child, speak to that young girl within. Bless that young child and affirm that God chose you before you were formed in the womb. (Jeremiah 1:5) God made you perfectly, unique and you are exactly who he called you to be. Now break every wrong word, attachment over your life and denounce every word of offense. Begin to speak life and that you are worthy, significant, special, loved, and appreciated. Write down words of affirmation about yourself to repeat daily in the mirror. Look at yourself and smile because you are exactly the person, the way God created you to be. You are accepted and more than enough because you were created by the enough.

Who AM I

I am created by God and chosen to do great and mighty things. I am worthy, blessed, significant, loved and more than enough. The fullness of God lives in me and created me for greatness. The purpose that God has placed within me shall prevail. I am exactly who God has called me to be. I shall walk in full potential because my father equipped me with greatness. I am a daughter (son) of the king. I am perfectly made, fully equipped, and exactly who God made me to be.

Cleansing Prayer

Lord, I make You Lord today of my mind, body, spirit and soul. I ask You to cleanse me from all residue of rejection, trauma, hurt and pain. I ask Lord that anything that is not like You be removed. Now Lord, Create in me a clean heart and a right mindset and make me whole again.

Forgiveness

Jesus, I thank you that you are a forgiving God. You took forgiveness to the cross so that we could be free. Lord, please forgive me and others who have done me wrong. (You may say names) I forgive _____ them for what they have done. I release the offense and occurrence to You. I lay all my hurt and pains at the alter. I go free now and forgive. Thank You, Lord, that I am released from all wounds, hurts, pains and remnants of the occurrence. I decree that every stronghold is released and I am set free and whole. I release bitterness, hurt, and every pain. I forgive myself for accepting the offense as well. Every UN-Godly Soul-ties are now broken and released now. I confess that I am FREE!

Vows

Lord, I confess that I have made self-imposed vows and I repent. I revoke any vow made and I revoke it and cancel the course of the vow. I no longer allow this vow to have a place in my life. I replace the vow with the blessing of the Lord. Now speak the word of the Lord, for the vow you made previously. (For example, a vow that you will never get married because you were hurt in a prior relationship)

Breaking Rejection

Lord, I repent for listening to the spirit that lied that I was not good enough, smart enough, loved, or inadequate. I repent for allowing myself to live in a false identity where rejection took root. I choose today to accept Your love and truth. I repent from any fears, doubts, and unbelief I have let in. I cancel every generational curse that is attached to me because of rejection. Lord, I ask you to show me my true identity. I now speak that

I am loved, significant, worthy, and made whole in Jesus Christ. I give myself permission to be free and become exactly who I am in Christ. I am favored, loved, worthy, significant, and blessed by God. I am enough.

Trauma Prayer

Lord, The pain from the trauma caused by _____ is hard and heavy right now. I know that your word says that you will turn it around for good. Lord, help me to heal from this pain and trauma. Lord, may You turn it around for good and use me to help others through this. Lord, thank You that You are the healing elixir and You heal every crevice and remnant so that I am made whole in You. Thank You Lord that trauma may have happened, but it will not deter my purpose.

Decrees

Offense

I now renounce any offense spoken over me, I am free from offense and I rebuke every word spoken that is not of God.

Worry

Lord, thank You that worry is not of You, I cancel worry from my mind and I go free to accept the thoughts of Christ.

Shyness

Lord, I think You that you created me Bold and with confidence, Today, I thank you that I walk fully in boldness and confidence from the origin which you created me.

Acceptance

Lord, I thank You that I am accepted by You, others and I accept myself as You see me.

Fear

Lord, thank You that You made me fear not, I am fearless and made in Your image to be great and walk in boldness.

Forgiven

Thank You Lord that You are a God of forgiveness, I receive your fullness of healing and forgiveness and it comes to me now.

Mind

Thank You Lord that my mind belongs to You, I declare that my thoughts are heavenly thoughts and shall correlate with heaven's blueprint.

Scripture

Romans 8:37 " I am more than a conqueror in Him. I am not alone; God is with me.

Deuteronomy 28:13 " I am the head and not the tail; I am above only and not beneath."

Colossians 1:11 " I am strengthened with all might according to HIS glorious power."

2 Timothy 1:7 " I do not have a spirit of fear, but a spirit of power, love and a sound mind."

Ephesians 6:1 " I am accepted in the beloved."

1 Corinthians 2:16 " But we understand these things, for we have the mind of Christ."

1 Corinthians 2:9 " However, as it is written, " What no eye has seen, what no ear has heard, and what no human mind has conceived" the things that God has prepared for those who love him.

Romans 8:14-16 " I am not an orphan. I am his child, for those that are led by the spirit are children of God."

Ephesians 3:20-21 " Now to him that is able to do exceedingly and abundantly above all that we ask or think.

Every situation that you have, God will exceed your expectations if you seek Him.

2 Corinthians 5:17 " Therefore anyone who is in Christ, is a new creation."

Your old life and old ways have passed away; you have a new identity that comes from Christ and your life is made new.

You are made to be strong, powerful, and Significant!

HE SAYS YOU ARE

Chosen, Queens, Kings, Sons, Daughters, Amazing, Incredible, Valuable, Important, Anointed, Called-Out, Faithful, Obedient, Gifted, Respected, Loved, Courageous, Determined, Radiant, Giving, His Masterpiece, Irreplaceable, Treasured, Priceless, A Jewel, Diamond, Supported, Loving, Creative, Kind, Honest, & Forgiving!

Decree Your Worth Daily

I am Powerful

I Am Wonderfully Made

I am Whole

I am Free

I am Healthy

I am Prosperous

I am Who God Says

I am Enough

I Walk In His Truth because I am His!

God Believes In You, & Wants You To Believe In You!

Today, Align your thoughts with Heaven's word

About You!

Blessings, Love,

& Wear Crazy Faith!

www.tespeaks.com

Your Purpose Motivator

Tiffany Ealy

PART II

The Teen Edition

Contents

Introduction

One very important scripture in the Bible that we should follow is one of the commandments: "Honor thy father and mother." While we don't get to choose our earthly parents, it is important to have gratitude and love towards them for their dedication in providing us with a good life and preparing us for the future. As children, we may not always agree with everything our parents say or the tasks they ask us to do, but it is crucial to respect and honor them due to their greater wisdom. It's worth remembering that they were once our age and experienced similar situations. With age, they have gained wisdom and learned from their own mistakes. Parents may also make decisions based on tradition because they were taught to do so. They follow the practices of their own parents, even though it may not always be the right way. Nevertheless, they strive to do their best in raising their children.

Always strive to study and gain knowledge in order to demonstrate your worthiness and understand the reasons behind events. Don't simply follow others or repeat the actions of your parents without comprehending the underlying motives. One of the gifts bestowed upon each of us by God is the power of choice. You have the freedom to make both right and wrong decisions. However, it's crucial to recognize that every choice you make carries consequences, and you must be prepared to accept and live with those outcomes. This is why it is vital to grasp the significance of God's plan for your life. Your spiritual father possesses complete knowledge of your earthly journey and desires to guide you towards prosperity within that plan. Conversely, the enemy also has a plan to disrupt God's intentions and prevent you from receiving the inheritance that rightfully belongs to you.

I'm writing this section of the book because life is filled with ups and downs. It is important to maintain a daily sense of motivation and arm yourself with knowledge to make sound decisions. By being aware of various truths, you can lead a healthier and more fulfilled life.

Let me be honest—I am far from perfect, and I have made my fair share of mistakes. However, my purpose in addressing you as a teenager is to empower you to make wise choices and spare you from years of walking around wounded and uninformed. When you experience healing, the opinions of those who fail to appreciate you become insignificant. You come to realize that your identity is defined by what God says about you.

Having a few loyal and genuine friends is far more valuable than being surrounded by a group of disloyal individuals with ulterior motives. Recognizing your own worth will lead you to be more intentional in various aspects of life. Our aim is to be in unity with God, but sin and opening doors to allow the enemy can push us further away from God's intended plan.

As a teenager, you are experiencing some of the most significant years of your life. This is a crucial time for self-discovery and understanding your true identity. The responsibilities of work and bills are not yet weighing on your shoulders, allowing you the freedom to focus on personal growth.

A quote that holds great importance and can be found in many of my books is, "If you don't know your true identity and worth, you will downgrade yourself and live below God's standards." This statement carries immense truth because when we are unaware of our identity, we allow others to define us through their actions, thoughts, and words. Instead of embracing who God created us to be, we believe the lies others tell us.

It's crucial to remember that people's opinions of you are just that—opinions. Often, others define us based on what others think of us, sometimes stemming from their own hurt and pain rather than a place of wholeness. It's important not to let these opinions define who you are or dictate your self-worth. True knowledge of your identity comes from understanding and accepting how God sees you

I recently reflected on what I would tell my younger self, and I wanted to share those insights. Firstly, I would say, "Don't let fear define you or hold you back from moving forward in life. Throughout your journey, you will encounter the word 'no.' Instead of being discouraged by it, see it as a valuable lesson and an indication that another door, perhaps even greater, is waiting to open for you. Sometimes, closed doors are meant to protect you and guide you towards better opportunities."

Secondly, I would emphasize the importance of not allowing anyone who did not create you to determine your worth and value. Understand that not everyone will like or appreciate you, and that's okay. The people meant to be in your life will accept and embrace you for who you are. It is essential to let go of negative influences and individuals who bring you down. Remember, you are not meant to please everyone, and your worth should never be dependent on someone else's opinion.

Lastly, as a young person, it is valuable to seek and discover your purpose in life. Take the time to understand why you were created and what brings you fulfillment. Focus on becoming the best version of yourself and finding wholeness before seeking to add others into your world. Your journey towards purpose and self-discovery is an individual process, and it's important to prioritize your own growth and well-being.

This way, you can be confident in who you are and not let others' opinions shake your sense of identity. It's important to remember that titles, status, and influence do not define your true worth. Many individuals who hold influence during high school, such as athletes or popular students, may not maintain that position once high school is over.

Additionally, it's worth noting that after high school, you may not regularly see or interact with many of your friends from that time. It's common for paths to diverge, and some of your high school peers may become distant memories. It's interesting to observe that those who were considered "nerds" or highly focused on their goals often end up being the most successful in the long run. The influence and trends that mattered in high school tend to lose their significance as you transition into adulthood.

You were anointed for greatness even before you were formed in your mother's womb. God had a clear understanding of your purpose and the unique journey you would undertake in your life. Your creator is the only one who truly knows the path that lies ahead for you. This realization is of utmost importance because seeking advice from those who are unaware of your calling or where you should be headed can be misleading.

Your purpose is exclusive to you, often hidden from the eyes of others. It resides deep within you, like treasures waiting to be discovered and utilized when the time is right. Once God activates your purpose, it may even be the first time that your parents recognize the remarkable gifts within you. That is why it is vital to seek guidance from the ultimate source, as others may not fully comprehend who you are and what you are meant to achieve. The enemy may employ friends or loved ones to discourage you from embracing the very purpose that God intends to bless you with.

You are destined to be an answer and a source of help to others through your purpose. The very challenges and burdens you have faced in your life can become powerful tools for aiding others. The areas where you have encountered the most difficulties and problems are often the places where God intends to work through you.

Pray continually and seek God in all aspects of your life. Ask Him about your purpose and what you should be doing at this moment. While it's important to enjoy your teenage years, also ensure that your decisions align with who God has called you to be. Every choice you make carries both spiritual and physical consequences. Whether your decisions turn out positively or negatively, there will be corresponding outcomes.

We often observe the physical consequences of our actions, but as teenagers, we may overlook the spiritual implications. It's essential to recognize that you are primarily a spiritual being inhabiting a physical body. Life's events and circumstances originate in the spiritual realm before manifesting in the physical world.

There are numerous things in the world that may appear right simply because they are popular or widely followed. However, the right way often diverges from the crowd and entails taking a narrow path. As a teenager, you are called to stand out and be a leader. When you choose not to follow misguided paths, you are making wise decisions that will positively impact your future and your future family.

God created both man and woman with the intention of marriage, where they come together to multiply and form a family. The union of a man and a woman is incredibly powerful when they join in unity to glorify God. Families have immense strength, and the synergy between a man and a woman in marriage can be truly impactful.

This is a reason why the enemy attacks our youth through homosexuality so our families would be compromised. From the beginning, God's blueprint for the family faced opposition, as our ancestors in slavery endured this assault. They valiantly struggled to remain united and honor the sanctity of marriage, recognizing the inherent strength within the family unit. However, in today's world, the entertainment industry and television perpetuate the notion that the family's significance is diminished or that it no longer requires the union of a man and a woman. Nevertheless, the fundamental design of the family remains unaltered, despite the world's attempts to persuade otherwise. Merely because society appears more accepting does not automatically validate its correctness. Departing from the divine design of the Kingdom deeply saddens our Father.

When we align ourselves with worldly ways, it creates an opportunity for sin to enter our lives and opens a door for the enemy. This distancing from God's plan occurs when we engage in sinful actions that establish a covenant with the enemy instead of with God. The presence of an open door allows the enemy access, and the covenant remains binding until it is spiritually broken.

God always grants us the freedom to choose whom we will serve. When we choose to follow worldly ways, we essentially worship the enemy. However, when we choose to worship God, we are covered by His redeeming blood, allowing us to pursue His divine plan for our lives. It is important to note that when the enemy establishes a door and covenant, God is obligated to honor that covenant. As a result, the fullness of His protective covering may be hindered due to the existing covenant.

By consciously choosing to align ourselves with God and break any ungodly covenants, we open ourselves to His abundant grace and protection. It is through this intentional decision to follow God's plan that we can experience His complete guidance and blessings in our lives.

There are multiple steps involved in the process of salvation. Accepting Christ is just one crucial step. It's important to understand that accepting Christ doesn't mean we will be exempt from life's challenges. In fact, we often grow and learn through the difficulties we face.

When we accept Christ and receive the Holy Spirit, our nature should undergo a transformation. Our choices and decisions should align with God's desires for our lives. This transformation should extend to our actions, as we strive to live in accordance with God's Word. We actively engage in acts of obedience, prayer, and fasting to align ourselves with God's perfect plans.

The journey of faith is not without its challenges, but it is a necessary path to receive the abundant blessings that God has in store for us. Throughout our lives, we encounter numerous significant decisions, and it is vital to include God in the process. Seeking His guidance and wisdom ensures that our choices lead to positive outcomes.

Moreover, when we have the Holy Spirit dwelling within us, our speech should reflect this transformation. We should refrain from using profanity and speaking words that are contrary to God's principles. Instead, our words should be characterized by love, kindness, and grace. The presence of the Holy Spirit should manifest in our language and interactions with others.

Different Forms
of Rejection

Rejection Form Opinions:

Life will throw dirt at you. You will go through things in life that try to knock you down and cause you pain. The main thing that matters is how you handle the situation. In every situation, God already has the answer. Remember that God knows your journey and is very aware of how you feel and what you are experiencing in life. For example, if someone calls you ugly or stupid, you have the power to speak up and say, "This is not who I am." Don't allow their opinion and lies to stick to you. When you allow a stigma to attach to you, you start to believe the lie about yourself. This will cause you to wear a mask on your face.

Then, you will begin to fear what others think and not truly show who you are. Instead of standing out, you will fall back. What I mean is that before you speak, you will start to wonder how others will perceive your words and whether they will accept you. This becomes an attack on your true purpose and worth, a direct assault on God's plan. It not only affects how you make decisions, but if you are not healed from those lies, it can also impact your future children. What remains unhealed in your life will continue to reside within you, growing deeper and deeper. Consequently, when more challenges come your way, it becomes harder to deal with those situations. This is because you now feel even more unloved, unappreciated, and unaccepted. A true friend will speak highly of you both to your face and behind your back.

(I want to emphasize the importance of this) It is crucial to remember that sometimes friends may act one way to your face while harboring jealousy behind your back. This does not align with the true definition of friendship. A genuine friend should genuinely desire the best for you, speak highly of you, and motivate you. They should display loyalty at all times. We are not perfect, and we all make mistakes, but a true friend remains authentic. The longer you take to heal from the opinions of others, the longer it will take for you to experience true freedom and live in accordance with your own truth. The world will only catch a glimpse of your wonderful personality, rather than truly getting to know you. Have you ever wondered why people say, "That person has changed"? Sometimes, change occurs when individuals find themselves and undergo a healing process. It is essentially the emergence of their true identity, with the removal of the mask they once wore.

Rejection after Parents' Divorce:

Thankfully, I lived with both of my parents until my father passed away when I was eight years old. I had many friends whose parents went through separation or divorce. Through this, I came to realize that a child experiences a tremendous amount of pain, similar to that of death. The child witnesses the constant bickering and arguing between their parents.

Divorce is a separation of your parents, and it is important to remember that it is not your fault. Furthermore, their decision to separate does not mean they don't love you. It signifies that they reached a point where they could not continue together and no longer had romantic love for each other. It's essential to recognize that marriage is often targeted by negative forces, which is why involving God in the equation is important.

You should still remain a major priority in both of your parents' lives. One of the challenges that many of my friends faced was that one parent missed significant milestones and memorable moments in their lives. The enemy will attempt to make you feel unloved, unappreciated, or left out in this process. Divorce brings about significant changes in your life and the lives of your parents. You now divide your time between two households that may have different routines and dynamics. Your parents are still dealing with the hurt and pain of the divorce, and healing is necessary for them.

Sometimes, in their own pain, parents may unintentionally hurt each other and attempt to involve the child in their conflicts. It is crucial to handle these situations with wisdom and remember that you are not responsible for their issues or conflicts.

Then, eventually, your parents may start dating again, and choosing a suitable partner becomes important. However, when you are still dealing with feelings of rejection and haven't fully healed, it can be challenging to make good choices in selecting a mate. The relationship your parent enters into may also have an impact on your own relationship with them. Remember, your life is significant to both your parents and to God. God hears your prayers and understands your true heart.

It is important to acknowledge that sometimes our parents have not fully healed from their own childhood rejections. This can influence their decision-making as adults and lead them to choose the wrong partner. When you carry unresolved rejection issues, you may often find yourself attracted to a mate who also carries similar wounds. That is why it is crucial to listen to God's guidance and allow Him to heal your own emotional wounds.

If these rejection issues are not addressed and healed, they can be passed down even before birth, affecting you as the child. If you do not find healing, the cycle of rejection can continue in your own family. Divorce may have been a recurring pattern in your family even before your parents' generation. Cycles of negative patterns can be perpetuated by familiar spirits, which attack marriages until they break. However, divorce is not the ultimate end, and it does not have to be your destiny. God desires for marriages to last until death, as there is great power and significance in the institution of marriage.

Rejection After Loss Of Loved One:

As I mentioned earlier, I lost my father at a young age. Dealing with the loss of a parent during that time was incredibly difficult. I couldn't help but think about all the significant life events my father would never be able to attend. I had countless questions I wanted to ask him, and I knew he would miss out on so many cherished moments. It's natural to desire both of your parents to be present to celebrate your milestones and offer guidance. Looking at my friends, I saw that they still had both parents in their households.

One of the biggest challenges I faced was the idea of having a stepfather figure in my life. As a young child, it's difficult to fully grasp the concept of loss. Your emotions are all over the place, and you navigate through them as you go along. Keeping your feelings bottled up inside doesn't truly help. It's crucial to have someone to talk to, and to seek solace in speaking with God. These can be immensely beneficial in so many ways. I was aware that my father was sick and experienced pain at times. I didn't want to witness his suffering, but I also didn't want him to be absent from my life. It's important to remember that healing is a day-by-day process, and with time, it becomes easier to cope and find healing.

Now, my mom didn't start dating immediately after my father's passing. It took years for her to heal and be ready to pursue romantic relationships. However, when she did start dating, it completely changed our lives. I felt like she was investing more time and attention into her relationships than she was with us. As a young child without a father, it was important for me to have a father figure in my life. Unfortunately, I didn't perceive any of the men my mother dated as father figures. Later on in life, I came to realize that when you carry unresolved rejection, it can lead you to make poor choices in romantic partners.

Later in life, I noticed that my mom made different choices in men compared to when I was a child. It made me realize that our parents can only parent based on what they have been taught themselves. Often, they may have also carried their own experiences of rejection from their own parents. I'm grateful that many of my friends had good parents, and their fathers served as positive examples of fatherhood.

Later in life, I came to understand that sometimes certain things must come to an end so that you can truly live. My father lived a purposeful life, albeit for a short time. It was his time to pass away, and yet I had to continue living and carry forward the torch of purpose. It's important not to let yourself wither away because a loved one has departed. One day, we will be reunited with them, but for now, we must persevere and live each day to the fullest. The journey is not easy, but God will provide healing and hold your hand through the difficult days. The pain and grief that death brings are indescribable. However, God eventually brings beauty back into your life. Things may never be the same, but what remains true is that God is still in control.

The cherished memories of the wonderful times are what you hold dear in your heart. Death is an inevitable part of life that we all must face, but your task is to live with purpose until that day arrives. Your purpose holds immense value, not only for yourself but also for others. It's crucial to keep moving forward because, by doing so, you open yourself up to the possibilities and blessings that await you.

No other person or relationship can fully complete you or fill the void left by loss. The only source of true healing for your heart and soul is God. It is necessary to seek God for healing, and through Him, love will be manifested through others, bringing restoration to your heart. In God, we find everything we need in life; He is capable of providing for all our needs.

Who Am I/ What Am I Saying

Words Are Important:

Words hold immense power as they have the ability to release blessings or curses. It is crucial to be mindful of the words you speak, both about yourself and others. Equally important is to pay attention to the words spoken over your life by others. You have the right to reject words that do not align with your true identity and purpose, and instead, embrace and celebrate the person God has created you to be.

At times, parents, friends, or loved ones may speak hurtful words in moments of anger or frustration. It's important to recognize that these words do not define you. You have the ability to rise above them and not let them shape your self-perception. Remember, the words of others do not have to become your reality. Unfortunately, this kind of situation occurs more frequently than we may think, but that doesn't make it acceptable.

I vividly recall a close acquaintance sharing an experience where a family member told them they would never amount to anything in life. Although they may have been somewhat mischievous as a child and gotten into some trouble, those were incredibly harsh words. Interestingly, we later observed how those words had an impact on them, but fortunately, they were able to find healing. It's essential to realize that such words can also affect the entire family. When we speak negative words over others, we risk attaching those words to our own family as well. Therefore, we must be mindful of our words and ensure they are filled with affirmation and blessings. If negative words manage to attach themselves, they can lead to stagnation and feelings of rejection.

Watch your choice of words when engaging in playful banter with others. Avoid using words that may cause rejection or negativity towards that person. Remember that our words have power, and even in lighthearted moments, the atmosphere doesn't differentiate between playfulness and seriousness. It's crucial to speak affirmations because they have a positive impact on our well-being. Affirmations, also known as decrees, celebrate our true selves and help us feel better about who we are. Verbal abuse is just as harmful as physical abuse, as it can have deep negative effects on a person. Bullying situations, including verbal abuse, can lead people to contemplate suicide because words of offense have the power to deeply wound and undermine someone's self-worth. It's essential to be mindful of the potential impact our words can have on others.

Any form of abuse, whether it's sexual, physical, or verbal, can result in rejection, hurt, and trauma. Verbal abuse, in particular, inflicts pain on the heart and inner soul, rather than the physical body. Each instance of verbal abuse leaves a hole in the inner soul, which continues to grow if left unaddressed. Eventually, the hole becomes so significant that it manifests as visible physical signs. This can manifest as rebellion, rejection, or the construction of emotional walls, as the child acts out in response to the feelings of rejection and hurt they experience.

Why do people develop a spirit of anger? It often stems from some form of hurt and pain they have experienced. If left unaddressed, this anger can grow and cause damage not only to themselves but also to others. Your words possess great power, so it's important to use them to nurture personal growth and uplift others. You wouldn't want your words to be the reason someone fails to embrace their purpose and feels rejected. Instead, strive to be an example by praying for others and speaking life into them. As you do so, your own life will flourish, and you will contribute to the growth and development of those around you. I recall my pastor emphasizing that a single word, touch, or divine action can shift your position and place you exactly where you belong. This could come directly from God or through the words and actions of others whom God uses to bless you. You are just one moment away from receiving and fulfilling what God has in store for you right now. Your words play a crucial role in propelling you forward in the right direction. They hold the power to unlock doors, but they can also lock someone's destiny with negative words. Choose your words wisely and avoid using the wrong key.

Names Are Important:

" And I will give to each one a white stone, and on that stone will be engraved a new name that no one understands except the one who received it.

{REVELATION 2:17}

" Before I was formed you in the womb I knew you, before you were born I set you apart"

{JEREMIAH 1:5}

The name that holds the utmost significance in our lives is Jesus. It is through the Blood of Jesus and the sacrifice made on the cross that we can experience a life of redemption and freedom. In biblical times, names were chosen carefully, and individuals often underwent name changes when they embraced their purpose. Names were a reflection of one's essence and the purpose they served, as well as their familial connections. In fact, some names were indicative of the experiences they had during those early days.

If you're unaware of the meaning behind your name, it's worthwhile to discover its true significance. In my case, my name signifies the manifestation of God. Once I grasped the meaning behind my name, I gained a deeper understanding of the purpose that God has bestowed upon my life. Additionally, my name is associated with jewels and value, which aligns with the message I convey in my books regarding identity and worth, as well as my endeavor to instill truth in others. This highlights the importance of one's name in shaping their future. Have you explored the meaning of your own name? I encourage you to research the characteristics and significance of your name to discern how they align with your purpose. As for nicknames, it is essential to choose positive ones that truly reflect who you are. Opt for nicknames that align with your purpose rather than derogatory ones such as "dog" or "killer." Before you were even brought into existence, God already knew your name and your purpose. This profound truth underscores God's comprehensive knowledge of every aspect of your life. It emphasizes the importance of seeking God in all things.

The words you choose to speak and the things you express should align with God's principles. In my own journey, I came to understand that the term "diva," often used to describe many women in our world, actually carries a demonic connotation, referring to the devil or a spirit that is worshipped. Furthermore, it can imply being spoiled or stuck-up, someone excessively focused on themselves. This word does not reflect godly values and is associated with witchcraft. It is crucial for us to be aware of the origins and meanings of the words we use. Many times, we encounter words in songs and lyrics that have demonic or negative origins. Therefore, we must exercise discernment and censor what we speak and listen to. Remember that you are a child of the Most High God and a citizen of His Kingdom. Do not allow the negative words of the world to define or influence you.

You are an integral part of the Kingdom, adopted as an heir alongside Jesus Christ. As you move forward in life, remember that you are never alone. God is with you, assisting you and residing within you, working towards perfection and personal growth. Your name is connected to divine promises, and it is essential for our minds to align with God's plans in order to understand them fully. When we allow fear to dominate our thoughts, we stray from God's perfect plan. Your name holds a divine purpose, as you are created in the image of the Father. Your life should reflect the thoughts and plans that God has established for you. The passage in Revelation mentioned above signifies a name change that occurs when we are saved and embrace our new nature in Christ. Salvation goes beyond simply accepting Christ; it involves transforming our old ways to align with God's divine ways. As we align our words, actions, and thoughts with the principles of the Kingdom, our lives begin to mirror our new nature. It is through this alignment that your unique identity emerges, bearing resemblance to the destiny in Christ that belongs to you.

Rejecting God's Plan

Rejecting Your Gift

" *But the man who had received one bag went off, dug a hole in the ground and hid his master's money.*

MATTHEW 25:18

I started this section off with the scripture of the talents. Please go and read the full scripture of the talents starting in verse fourteen. This scripture is significant in speaking about your gifts. It's not just about money, but also about hiding what God has placed within you. God has given you gifts that belong to and are significant to you. The gifts are hidden inside of you like treasures until it's time for their intended use. This is why we don't know our purpose automatically.

God places your gift inside of you until it's time to reveal it. Others may have a gift that resembles yours, but the influence of using the gift can't be duplicated. This gift is not only important to you but also to your offspring and the people you are assigned to bless and influence.

Imagine a line of people waiting for a concert. They are waiting for you to walk in your purpose and unlock their potential to move forward. They need you in that line. Someone is assigned to help you on your journey, and you are assigned to help many on theirs.

When God shows you your gift, He wants you to use it and not hold onto it. He is ready to reveal your gift to the world when He allows you to use it. When you reject your gift, you reject God and who He made you to be. You place God in a box and say that you can't do it, but you don't realize that you can because God is doing it through you. God attracts people to your gift so that He can get the glory. He is the one drawing people to your gift, not you. When you worry about how others will see you, you diminish God and place others as idols before Him. Fear places God in a box and limits you from going forth in your gift. We limit God's greatness when we fail to cultivate and operate in His gifts. Don't let fear be the reason that you don't go forth. The enemy wants you to fear because fear can keep you stagnant and attempt to steal what God has placed in you.

For example, I remember when I started writing my first book. I knew it was a gift from God because He started placing ideas and titles into my spirit. I had a lot of fear wondering who would support me, who would like my books, and whether they would be successful.

Now, if God gave it to you: (1) it will be successful and blessed, (2) it is for a purpose to help others, and (3) there will be testing and a journey, and you will have to remain grounded and remember His promise. The one thing we must remember is that success doesn't come instantly. You may begin your purpose, and many things will test you and cause you to doubt yourself and God's plan. We must remember that success is not instant.

The journey is necessary, and we must stay aligned with our purpose to see the promise. Things will die in your life, physically and spiritually, along the way. You will see your friends change, and you will have to let go of certain behaviors to achieve another level. In the end, the entire journey is necessary, including the full process. Knowing your true worth and identity comes from God, which allows you to not fall to man's opinion. Many will question why you write or why you do what you do. Even your parents may not be able to understand God's purpose until they see the blessing of the purpose. If you stop because of others' opinions, you cannot fulfill your purpose. God placed the purpose in you, but He did not share it with everyone. He wants others to see you walking in your purpose.

I finally came to realize that disobedience and rejecting God's gift is a form of sin. I had to repent for sitting on my gift and not moving according to God's plan. You are sitting on a gift that is supposed to produce wealth in your life and help others. The gift is significant to you, and no one else can provide it but God. This is so important because it didn't come from your friends or parents. God gave you gifts that your parents may have as well, but they come directly from God, and they belong to you. We shouldn't diminish our greatness to gain the approval of others or let others disapprove of our gifts. Fear should not be our position, and it should not have a place in our lives. God has given us boldness and confidence when we learn to align with his presence within us.

You have the ability to use your gift because God is with you, guiding you along the way. However, walking in purpose can be challenging, and the enemy may try to derail you from your journey. You may lose some friends and encounter obstacles, but your obedience is crucial for fulfilling your purpose and blessing others. Remember, your gifts are not just for you, but for others as well. Along with your gifts, God anoints you with influence to impact others' lives.

It's important to understand that you may not see the full picture of your purpose, but God's promises never fail. Don't let your natural perspective hinder your spiritual understanding. Your gift will open doors and create opportunities, so don't give up! Keep pushing forward, and you will see the fulfillment of God's plan for your life. Even those who doubted you will witness the truth of God's work in your life. Although you may not always be able to trust those around you, you can always trust in God's perfect track record. His plan for your gifts is unbreakable and unwavering.

One of my childhood friends had a daughter who battled Lupus. During her battle, she used her gift of writing to journal, encourage others, and raise awareness about Lupus. Despite knowing that she may not live to see many things in her life, she understood that part of her purpose was to help other young teens battling Lupus be encouraged and come to know God. She pushed herself daily to write and encourage so many teens. Unfortunately, she went to be with the Lord at the early age of 24, but she had asked her mom to make sure others knew her story and to continue to give events about Lupus. I attended one of the events, and there was a young lady who wanted to meet Kaishall, but it was too late. Kaishall had passed the week before the meeting. The young lady was heartbroken, but she wanted Kaishall's mom to know how much Kay had inspired her. This touching story made me realize that if Kay could touch so many lives while being sick, how many more lives can we touch with our own gifts and purposes.

Why can't we walk in purpose if we don't have any sickness keeping us down? Kay's mother later honored her daughter's wishes and continued to hold Lupus awareness celebrations in honor of Kay. She also documented Kay's journey in a book about her experiences. Today, know that you can be a Kaishall for someone who needs your story to inspire them and help them reach the next level. Do it for God, do it for yourself, do it for Kay, and do it for all those you are assigned to reach. The very thing that comes against you is the area where God wants to bless and use you. I hope this true story about Kay's strength and resilience during her sickness inspires you to keep moving forward. You can read more about Kay's story on her webpage doitforkay.com. Her mother has done an excellent job keeping her daughter's journey alive and she is a loving and outstanding example to others. Kay's mother has taken up the torch to continue the purpose that was started by her daughter. Death can often open up a purpose you never knew existed.

Bullying:

I chose to address the topic of bullying in this book because it's an issue that many young kids encounter during their school years. I recall a particular instance where a young lady who was overweight would bully other children for their food. She had a love for eating but felt ashamed of her size, and it seemed like she bullied others to prevent them from bullying her. However, bullying is never an acceptable way to deal with one's insecurities. It's important to recognize the impact of our words, as they can not only affect others but can also come back to us or our loved ones. It's essential to operate in a Godly manner and treat others with kindness and respect. With time, that young lady learned to control her weight and embarked on a health journey. It's worth noting that many individuals have had their lives negatively impacted by bullying, and we must address this issue and promote a culture of kindness and empathy.

Bullying is a tool used by one person to exert control over another. It's often fueled by the bully's own insecurities, just like the young lady I mentioned earlier whose weight was a source of shame for her. We must not allow anyone to control us, nor should we accept negative words spoken by others. As children, we may need the guidance of an adult to help us navigate these situations. As I got older, I realized that bullies do not recognize the inherent value of every human being as a Child of God. They are being used by the enemy to degrade and belittle others and to make them feel less than what God created them to be.

That bully doesn't know if you will become the next minister, president, attorney, or doctor. The bully is sent to stagnate and kill your destiny. In life, you will always have people who are used by the enemy to come against the anointing and purpose in your life. This is why it is important not to allow others to define your worth or steal your identity. Your future is based on who God has called you to be, not on titles or income. Things can change in an instant, as someone who has just been laid off can attest to. You can be up one minute and down the next. Your virtue doesn't come from others, but from God who has made you who you are. Can you remain the same person with or without success and titles? You are made for greatness, and no one can define you but God. Remember that your worth doesn't change based on circumstances or pain; you are always valuable to God.

The best part is that God will heal your broken areas so that you can walk in your truth and identity. We are all damaged goods because of the dirt that gets thrown on us and the hurt and pain we may go through. However, we have freedom in God and our righteousness in the Father. Our circumstances are meant to teach us, help us grow, and allow us to help others through our testimony.

Untie The Knot

UnGodly Ties:

" *Therefore a man shall leave Gus father and mother and the two will become one.*

EPHESIANS 5:31

In life, we will meet many people, including seasonal friends, long-term friends, and romantic partners. When you spend time with someone in a relationship, you become tied to that person or get closer to them. Some ties to your friends or partner are godly, while others may not be. Soul ties create an emotional, spiritual, and physical connection with someone else. You can form a soul tie with friends, parents, partners, and other people you have a relationship with, as you form a bond with those you are close to.

Sometimes, these bonds can become controlling or demonic in nature. When we bond with others, we form a connection with them. If you become deeply connected with someone and place them as an idol (worship them more than God), it is ungodly. Seeking advice from someone who is not godly means you are placing them before God. God does not like to be second to anyone. When we form bonds with others, they can influence our decisions and thoughts. We may not know who they worship or what they allow into their lives that is not of God.

Consider a situation where you formed a bond with a friend, and you did everything together. Then, suddenly, you found out that they were not a loyal friend, and they started gossiping about you to others. This relationship is certainly a soul tie that needs to be severed. When we sever a soul tie, we must repent to God and cancel the connection spiritually, so that our soul is healed from any unholy attachment to that person. It is important to forgive the friend for what they have done, but you don't have to reinstate the friendship with that person. Sometimes, God may remove friends from our lives because he knows they are not a good fit for us. Some friends are only seasonal and are not meant to follow us into the future. Your future is important to God, and unholy soul ties can affect you in the future.

Now, let's consider a situation where you dated someone and formed a close bond with them. You would talk on the phone for hours, and you might even fall asleep on the phone together. As you talk multiple times a day, you start to develop feelings for this person. You hug, kiss, and may even engage in sexual activity with them. This bond goes beyond friendship and creates a soul tie.

Unholy soul ties are certainly formed when there is sex before marriage. I remember my mother telling me in high school, "Don't come home with a baby." She would also tell my boyfriends to bring me back the way they found me, which meant not coming back with a baby. When you engage in sex before marriage, you form a covenant bond with that person. You become physically, emotionally, and spiritually attached to them. This means that whoever you or your partner slept with is also attached to both of you. Their emotions, what they worship, and what they do and feel are all attached to you as well.

This is why it can be difficult to break free from an abusive relationship, even though you know it is not good for you. The unholy soul tie that has been formed makes it hard to let go. It is important to cancel and release the spiritual soul tie so that it does not continue to have a hold on your soul. Soul ties can be a form of bondage, and they will remain attached unless they are spiritually broken and removed. This is one of the reasons why God created marriage, for a man and woman to form a bond and produce offspring. When 1+1 come together, they multiply and produce fruit. If you engage in sex multiple times before marriage, your partner may have other covenants and associations with other partners, which can lead to emotional and spiritual entanglements.

Every person you engage in sexual activity with creates a soul tie that can have both positive and negative effects. A soul tie can be positive when it brings two people closer to God's plan, but it can be negative when it causes one to deviate from it. In marriage, a soul tie forms a strong bond between the couple, making them act and look more alike. This is because the bond knits them together as one. However, if a person is carrying demonic baggage or has a demon attached to them, these things can also transfer. This is why people's behaviors can change, as they reflect who they are sleeping with.

If you believe you are attached to any ungodly soul ties, ask the Holy Spirit to remove the covenant of those soul ties from your soul. Repent of the soul tie as well. If you fail to sever a harmful soul tie, it can affect future relationships and decisions in your life. Remember, you may have multiple people attached to your soul from the person you are tied to and who they are attached to as well. This is a major reason why you may keep attracting the same type of behavior to you. You may have some rejection issues or soul ties that are still attached. You always want to sever any unholy ties and heal before starting a new relationship with someone.

Remember that if you don't break free from unholy ties, you will continue to experience the same negative cycles. Always make careful decisions about who you allow into your life, whether it's friends or romantic relationships. God intends for you to connect with people who are aligned with His plan for your life, including potential future spouses. Casual hookups and forming bonds with just anyone can have negative consequences on your joy, future, and overall well-being. You are valuable and deserving of making good choices about who you allow into your space. Choose friends wisely and be selective about potential mates who exhibit qualities of husband material. Keep in mind that unholy soul ties can affect not only you but also your future offspring if not addressed and healed.

While I have never had an abortion, I have had friends who have. I understand that as a young person, if you get pregnant, some teens choose abortion so they do not have to tell their parents. Secondly, they may not be ready to have a baby and become a teen parent. As a teen, you think differently than an adult when it comes to making life choices. However, most adults make better decisions because they have experience and wisdom.

As a teen, I never thought of abortion as murder, but I knew it was not right. God has ordained who you are before you were even in your mother's womb. This means that even a fetus at that stage has a purpose that God has ordained. It is murder to kill and abort a baby. As a teenager, you may not consider this as murder, and your approach to getting rid of a baby may differ from that of an adult. However, what most people do not know is that there are spiritual consequences to abortion.

Let me explain in more detail. When blood is shed on the table, an established covenant is made. A covenant can be good or bad. However, this covenant is not with God, but with a demon of abortion called Molech. It is important to cancel and repent for this covenant because an abortion spirit can become attached to your future. Physical illnesses and future plans may be aborted before they come to fruition due to the act of abortion that was committed. This may cause some people to wonder why they cannot finish things.

At times, an abortion spirit may be present. You are primarily a spiritual being residing in a physical body, which implies that whatever occurs in the physical realm originates in the spiritual realm. When you enter into a binding covenant, whether it is Godly or demonic, it has a significant impact. To prevent the curse from influencing your life, it must be broken spiritually. Curses may attach themselves to both you and your children. Often, if a parent has had an abortion, the negative patterns may continue down the family line and affect the child. You always have the power to make choices that will affect you. Numerous choices made by our parents and ancestors continue to affect us in our lives, despite the fact that they were not our responsibility. Knowledge opens the door for us to make informed decisions.

In some instances where the baby has infirmities that will not allow survival, God recognizes that it is not your fault if doctors must abort the fetus. However, in all cases, we should pray and seek understanding of the spiritual and physical consequences of our important decisions. God will always provide peace in our decision-making process. When we do sin, we should quickly repent and turn away from that sin to avoid repeating it.

Do not return to what caused you pain and abuse. Going back may prevent progress in your future. Although moving forward may be difficult, you can always pray for assistance. Just like food, relationships have an expiration date, and it is unwise to consume rotten food. Similarly, expired relationships can become unpleasant and harmful. Do not hold on to what does not belong to you, as it may hinder your progress. We must often disconnect from the past before God can guide us to our next stage.

At times, it is necessary to block numbers and remove oneself from availability. When God removes things and people from your life, view it as a lesson, as He always acts in your best interests. Although it may be painful initially, you will eventually comprehend the rationale behind it. You can always trust that God's track record shows that He intends the best for you, not evil. That's why it's essential to stay grounded in the Word and comprehend its knowledge. Every decision you make, whether good or bad, has an impact on your future and that of your offspring. As a child, most of your life choices are made by your parents, but as a teenager, your choices directly influence your life both now and in the future. Your current actions, the people you let into your life, and the priorities you set will determine your future.

Rejected By Associations

When we join associations or organizations, there are often rules and covenants that need to be signed. Wherever you enter into agreements or invest your money, you align with the standards of the organization or association. In the past, I aspired to join a Greek organization, but I wasn't selected, and it was disheartening. However, I later realized that this wasn't God's plan, and my desire to be a part of that organization vanished. As I matured, I came to understand that joining an organization often means forming a covenant that may not align with God's values.

The first Greek organization was founded in 1776 by a college student studying Greek. He had been rejected by two secret societies on campus and decided to establish his own Greek organization. This piece of information caught my attention because this book is about rejection. As I continued to read, I came across a few articles from individuals who had left Greek organizations as they felt led by God.

I further thought about how many organizations reject applicants based on their status, skin color, associations, and other factors. Additionally, hazing, the initial process, and the rules they follow can also go against God's standards. When I think of organizations branding letters on their members, it reminds me of the branding of animals during slavery. Some organizations brand letters or pictures on their members, and sometimes blood is shed. This is another covenant that is made, and we accept many things simply because they are popular, but many of these covenants are unholy.

I am not saying that all associations and organizations are unholy, but many of them worship other gods. When you make a decision to join a group, read the rules and do research on the organization. Make sure that you are making a covenant that is Godly and aligns with who you are. Your purpose is not just a purpose that you have in this world, but you have a God purpose, and that is why you exist. If any association does not align with God's plan and purpose, you should consider not joining.

One thing I've learned in life is that quality relationships and bonds are better than quantity. It is better to have solid foundations and relationships than to have multiple associations that may hinder God's plan. Always seek God in every decision, pray and research before making any decisions about where you invest your time, money, and agreements. As a young teen, it is essential to spend your time wisely and on things that add value to your life. Don't forget to give a portion of your time to the Creator. You are important to Him, and He wants you to excel. God should always come first in all that you do. The right relationships and connections that God wants to divinely be a part of your life, He will place in your life. Always remember to pray and ask God to show you His vision for your life, and you will always make the right decision.

Classiness Over Lust:

As a teenager, it's natural to want to keep up with the latest trends and popular fashion. You want to be acknowledged, noticed, and complimented on your appearance. It's understandable that you want the latest shoes, clothes, hairstyles, and makeup to be on point. However, we need to remember that our bodies are temples of God and we need to respect them. When we dress in revealing clothing, we attract lustful attention, which is temporary and attracts men who only want sex. Men want a woman who is covered up and classy, not one who shows off her body to everyone.

Classiness is timeless and beautiful. A man who wants to love you from the inside out will be attracted to your classiness. A woman who dresses with modesty and respect will attract an honest and honorable man who sees her as wifey material. On the other hand, men often lust after women who dress provocatively, but they don't view them as potential life partners.

Remember that you were created to stand out and be respectful. You are not meant to fit in with the crowd, but to step into the room differently and stand out from the crowd. When you operate like the crowd, the right man won't see you because you look like and resemble the crowd. You can still be classy and tasteful while also being sexy. The world may tell you that sex sells, but it only sells lust and unholy ties and attachments.

You are made to be someone's wife and mother if you desire to have children. Dress to impress the future job you want and the future spouse you want. Dress to impress so that your future husband/wife says that there is something about you that stands out. Your future mate should recognize you by your presence and not by your lack of clothing. The Bible says that "he who finds a wife finds a good thing and obtains favor from the Lord." You are a man's favor. You are fully equipped already as a wife, mother, prayer warrior, and everything that God has called you to be. Your gifts need to be cultivated, but they already exist. The more time you spend with God, the more oil He pours into your life.

Moving In Purpose

From Rejection to Purpose:

There are many things that God has called you to do in life. You have an important purpose connected to you, and God has connected you to do great things even before you were born. Although others may have a similar purpose, they cannot do it like you can. Your purpose has a unique piece that allows you to do it differently and with greatness. You are uniquely made with greatness on the inside of you. God has given you the confidence and boldness to walk in that purpose.

The gift that God has placed inside of you has a unique blueprint in heaven, written with your name and a full journey of chapters. You have a book in heaven that outlines your entire life journey, and it belongs to you. God unlocks the pages of your book and equips you to fulfill your divine purpose. However, in life, we are given a choice to follow God's way or the world's way. Some things may come easily to us and we are able to do them with ease. But when rejection or blockages come from the enemy, they can cause us to stagnate and prevent us from moving towards our destiny. The enemy tries to block our true destiny from evolving on earth. Therefore, we will go through a process of growing, learning, and testing in our purpose.

When I first started writing, I began as God wanted me to. However, I put the book down many times due to fear of the unknown. This was a choice I made because I let fear take over for a while. Oftentimes, the greatest things are built and birthed in our pain. Your purpose is actually a spiritual birthing process. Just like your physical mother went through a birthing process with many pains and a nine-month journey, your promise and purpose have a birthing journey, and the pains help you to stand in times of adversity. God wants you to reach the mountain and fulfill your full promise, but in order to get there, there are also periods of testing, adversity, and obstacles that will be thrown in your path. When adversity comes against our purpose, we must focus on the promise and not the problems. When you keep going and follow God's plan, you become a dangerous force against the enemy.

The enemy attacks your mind with wrong thoughts in order to derail you from following God's plan. But you have power over your thoughts and what you allow into your mind. Your mind is a powerful tool and your words hold great influence. The things you meditate on most will affect the decisions you make. It's important to choose positive music and television shows that feed your soul. In the past, I didn't pay attention to the lyrics of songs, only the beat. But now, I listen to both. I've realized that many things in the world try to plant the wrong seeds in our lives. God wants us to nourish our souls with good food, good music, and good movies that help us grow and make good choices. The wrong seeds can be planted because many people are willing to sell their souls for money and the desires of the world. That's why it's essential to feed your soul with purposeful things and seeds of growth that will produce a good harvest.

There are divine connections, mentors, and connectors that God has called you to connect with for your purpose. These people God has placed in your life to help thrust you and move you into your purpose. The relationships God brings into your life are two-fold. This means that you are meant to help them, and they are meant to help you. We should never stop learning because destiny helpers come even to you as an adult. You have to be willing to invest not only money in yourself but also time. We must prepare for what belongs to us. This means that you should seek to learn about the career you want, research, study, and prepare. What you spend the most time on is what you will be great at.

For instance, athletes practice their sport for many hours, and the more they practice, the better they become. God will bring mentors into your life who will help you, but you also need to be prepared to help others. Always seek to pay it forward when you can. Your divine purpose is to help others and make money. Don't think of yourself as being in competition with others. There will always be someone who does what you do, but God has called you to do it differently and be great at it. Your purpose is to help others and bring them closer to completion through your unique talents. If God has done it for others, he will do it for you too. When God places a purpose within you, he will also bless you.

I remember having a dream where I was flying at an incredibly high speed and altitude, so much so that it felt overwhelming. I realized that God was showing me a vision of my future. In the dream, I grabbed my husband's arm and stood still as the speed increased, and we ascended even higher. Your purpose is like a flight to an unknown but wonderful destination. Imagine yourself on this flight, with a clear plan and aspirations in mind. Write down the places you want to travel to and the goals you want to achieve. Also, consider the people you want to have on this journey with you. Your destiny is a perfect and unique destination, written just for you.

God has a blueprint for your destiny, which is like the highest peak you can reach. He is the pilot in your flight of destiny, and the journey is fully planned by Him. Although there may be delays, problems, and storms along the way, you will reach your destination if you stay focused on God's plan. Your journey is a part of your inheritance, and you must align your words, actions, and movements with His Word at all times. Don't let disappointment and the words of others stop you or distract you from your destination. The distractions come to deter and delay your full flight and arrival, but when they come, keep praying, praising, believing, and trusting His plan. Your journey is already in mid-air, and you will have many stops along the way that are a part of the journey. Pray and ask God to release the blueprint and instructions for your flight.

Don't give up and don't give in to the enemy's devices. Your flight will arrive on time and everything that belongs to you will come forth. Your life has been marked by purpose, prophecy, and a divine journey. Once you understand that God's plan is the best and the right plan, you will know which direction to go in. However, the journey will not be easy, and there will be storms that arise. But we must always remember that God is with us, and he knows the full and exact journey. He knows the beginning and the end, so he knows what is best for us. You have a choice to move with God and his plans, which are likely different from your own plans.

The next option is to follow your flesh, which is the enemy's plan. One choice leads to an abundant life, while the other choice can lead you to many open doors where the enemy is in control of your actions and life. In the book of Proverbs 19:21, it says, "Many plans are in a man's mind, but it is the Lord's plan and purpose that will stand (come to pass)." Whose plan will you choose to follow today? Remember, God is always in control, even when it doesn't seem like it. He is moving right now behind the scenes to complete and bring his word in your life to pass. Keep seeking God and don't give up. The plans of God over your life shall prevail, and they are always for your good.

Illustration of God's Refining Power:

One night, we needed to replace a piece of equipment on our clothes dryer. As my husband dismantled a portion of the dryer to clean the residue, dirt, and lint fell out. It was at that moment that God gave me a revelation. He showed me that the things that have hindered us and created strongholds inside of us are like dirt. They are everything that has come against our destiny to try and stop us from moving forward. This includes pain, rejection, trauma, times of being told no, worries, fear, unbelief, words of offense, and other things in life that have attempted to take us out of alignment with God's will. These things build up and fill up in our soulish area. God gave me an illustration that they were like stink bugs - those nasty bugs that stink badly when you step on them or kill them. Our insides become dirty and stinky and need to be cleaned to realign us with God's purpose.

The clothes dryer gets so hot that it transforms the clothes from wet to a state of dryness. This is how God works within us. His transforming power is like a refining fire that removes the residue and dirt within us. He melts away all the stinky things and dirt so they can no longer affect us. Then, our insides are purified by the water and blood.

As you continue to seek God and stay in His presence, He is able to anoint your head with oil, and you will be transformed by His spirit within you. The more you seek Him, the more transformation occurs, and He is able to use you to your fullest potential. The Spirit within you, which is your new nature, helps to eliminate the old things that hindered you in the past. This new you is then able to help transform other people's lives. When you feel inadequate, you need to fully seek God, who is more than enough. You are made in His image and are enough just as you are. God is the one who can heal you from the "dirt" in your life. Sometimes, we try to find healing in the wrong places, but true and lasting healing only comes from God. He is the one who completes and refines the broken areas of our lives, making us whole. He is the master builder of our lives, and when something feels missing, seek God to help heal and make you whole again.

Illustration 2 Turn the Pages of the Book:

As a writer/scribe, I'd like to use a book as an analogy for life. Imagine your favorite book, where you read it over and over again. Just like in a book, some chapters in life may be boring, while others may be great. Some chapters are meant for learning, teaching, and growing, while others are filled with trials. In your life, you must trust God even in the chapters where life seems to be throwing dirt and lemons at you. God will eventually use those chapters to make lemonade and reveal who you truly are. The bad chapters are where you are made, and you grow in your struggles. The good chapters show you that God can use your worst moments to create a beautiful story.

You must keep moving, thriving, and discovering yourself to get to the best chapters. Your life is always evolving, growing, and changing, and it doesn't stop until God says it does. Don't let what others have done or said about you stop you from living. The only one who can live and define your life is you and God. Even your parents can only guide you through and teach you lessons, but ultimately, it's your journey to take. Allow God to be the focus of your divine journey because His version is always the best version. Your story is being written now, so allow God to turn your pages and build your journey.

New Age Practices (Not of God):

Sometimes, systems and rules can lead us to believe that there is more than one God. However, there is only one God that governs all - His Kingdom. Denominations and religions are man-made, not created by God. They are often used to control people, but God wants us to know how to access His Kingdom on Earth. We must worship the true God and study to know and seek Him for ourselves. The Church is not a building, but rather, we are the Church. When we gather together in a church home, the atmosphere should reflect the spirit and nature of God. It is through this unity that we see the miracles, signs, and wonders of God.

Astrology is not a means of predicting your personality or future. You are made in God's image with a divine purpose, and the stars cannot determine that purpose. New agers who claim to be connected to the Kingdom of Light are, in fact, connected to the Kingdom of Darkness.

Worshipping other gods such as the Sun, Moon, Cosmos, Scientology, Witchcraft, etc., is not godly and goes against God's will. We must remain faithful to the one true God and not be swayed by false beliefs or practices.

Reincarnation, Sage, Yoga, Chakara (started in Hinduism), Acupuncture, crystals, Beads. Ouija Boards, Mediums, Psychics (they worship the dark side to get results) and this is witchcraft. You have to sacrifice something to obtain a result. Not Godly.

Law of attraction - Your full reward is in heaven, what belongs to you is already in heaven and you can pull down your blessing from heaven to Earth. You are a spiritual being first. **Matthew 6:33** Seek ye first the Kingdom of God, and his righteousness and all these things shall be added unto you.

Illustration Three:

You've just poured a glass of cold water into your favorite glass. You drink it, and your thirst is quenched. Similarly, in life, various people such as television and movie characters, pastors, parents, and friends can influence the choices you make. While parents and adults carry wisdom, some traditions may not be beneficial. Therefore, it is essential to make decisions based on what is right. Be cautious of who mentors or teaches you, the media you consume, and the company you keep, as they significantly impact your decisions. Invest in yourself and take time to seek God's guidance in every decision. Just as you drink water from a trusted source, ensure that you're influenced by the right sources in your life.

Discovering Purpose:

- What do you do with ease, and love doing and probably would do for free?

- What are your skills that you see as a gift and you do better than others?

- What do others complement you on doing?

- What area are you tested in and see attacks against?

- What subjects do you love and school?

- What do you spend your free time doing?

- What makes you happy?

- What business would you start if you had the money and nothing would stop you?

Your purpose and the plan God has for you costs more than the money you will have in your hands. Most people don't know how it will happen or when. Only God knows the full story. When you take one step, God will open doors of favor and opportunity. When you are obedient to God fully; he will move the mountains in your life.

Quotes

" Look at every failure as a stepping stone to your victory. It is along your journey to add value. Don't give up."

" If it didn't work, trust God that he wants to provide better."

" Write down and make your goals plain. Draw up your action plain. Ask God to reveal his blueprints and instruction about your purpose."

" Dress for success and the position you want. Classy is better than dressing lustfully."

" Keep great motivators around you that will thrust you and motivate you to keep moving."

" Be obedient and the favor of God will follow.

" *Declare words of promise over your life and speak blessings daily."*

" *Don't gossip and don't speak negative your words create over you and others."*

" *Don't change yourself to suit others, you are made to stand out and be great."*

" *Don't lower your standards because when you lower your standards you will keep accepting less in your life."*

" *Never allow yourself to be second, you are not made to be a side mate."*

" *Loyalty is important in friendships and lasting relationships."*

" *You are not made for mediocrity, but for greatness. Plow deep, discover, accomplish and prosper. God engineered you for victory."*

" *When you tap into Christ's full design for your life you become Powerful, strong, and unstoppable.*"

" *Do alone what you would do in front of others; God sees all and knows all.*"

Letter to a Young Queen

Dear young queen, one day you will blossom into a beautiful woman. Even now, you are being molded into the person God created you to be. Along the way, many people will come and go, and you'll have to make choices that affect your future. Inside of you lie gifts that God will bring forth in due time. They are yours to cultivate and use to fulfill your unique purpose. Don't be afraid to stand out and make choices that may go against the crowd.

You'll have good days and bad days, but remember to keep a positive attitude and lean on God. Your praise is a powerful weapon, especially on difficult days. If you make a mistake or a wrong choice, repent and learn from it. God will use even your mistakes for your growth and to help others.

When you feel alone, remember that God is always with you, guiding you through the Holy Spirit. Your worth and identity don't come from the world or people around you, but from the fact that you were made in God's image. You are special, worthy, and powerful with a unique purpose. Don't let anyone make you feel otherwise. Keep shining, young queen.

You were born as a queen to be respected and treated as such. Don't allow anyone who did not create you to define or disrespect you. Circumstances, people, and things will try to deter you from being all God has called you to be. It is up to you to believe in the promise God has placed within you and not give up. Dirt will be thrown at you, and sometimes it may make you cry. However, God sees your tears and He will turn your worst moments into better ones. Remember to speak positively because your words activate God and the angels to move. Also, align your actions with what God has spoken regarding your future. When we make negative moves or speak negatively, we are moving away from God.

Who you hang around with, the choices you make, and your actions will all determine what you see come to pass in your life. Always remember to pray often, fast, praise, and surround yourself with like-minded individuals. Popularity is not always the way to go in life. What seems popular in the world is not necessarily what is seen by God as success and goodness. The world places a price tag on things to make them seem popular and attractive. Titles, high-end items, and others' opinions do not define you. Making the right choices and moving in the plans of God's will for your life always advances you. You are meant to stand out and be different, and that is a good thing.

Your divine future has already been written by God before you were born. The dreams and ideas God provides to you are given in small portions. There will be people God places to connect with you and help you move in purpose, and there will be some who try to deter you from your purpose. You must recognize who God has placed in your life and look for those who will celebrate you instead of talking and gossiping about you. You are not meant to be defined by a certain title or money. You are exactly who God says you are and meant to operate in greatness.

This book was written to help you understand your spiritual side and how it affects your natural world. It is okay to not be liked or understood by everyone. You will be celebrated by the right people. Remember to always seek God first in all that you do. What belongs to you will come. I pray that this book helps you bypass some of the mistakes and wrong choices that can hinder your purpose. When we lack knowledge, we can't make informed decisions. You always have a choice of which way you want to go, but each choice decides your future and outcome. I pray, young queen, that your choices will be guided by truth and not the world. May the Holy Spirit's guidance begin to mark your life with the blueprints of heaven over your life.

"*I Am Everything That God Says, Now*"
"*Live Your Destiny, Not Your Rejection!*"

TESPEAKS

Your identity & truth are anchored in God! I decree you are Significant, More Than Enough, & Exactly Who God Says Now! I pray that this book blessed, healed and brought you closer to the father. You can get more of my books and your Live your destiny t-shirts @ my webpage tespeaks.com. I am available for speaking engagements, and book signings; please contact tiffanyealyspeaks@gmail.com.

www.ingramcontent.com/pod-product-compliance
Lightning Source LLC
Chambersburg PA
CBHW060324130626
46553CB00003B/914